Bluffer's®

GUIDE TO
CYCLING

ROB AINSLEY

© Haynes Publishing 2018
Published June 2018

A CIP Catalogue record for this book
is available from the British Library.

ISBN: 978 1 78521 228 4

Library of Congress control no. 2018932886

Published by Haynes Publishing,
Sparkford, Yeovil, Somerset BA22 7JJ
Tel: 01963 440635
Int. tel: +44 1963 440635
Website: www.haynes.com

Printed in Malaysia.

Series Editor: David Allsop.
Front cover illustration by Alan Capel.

CONTENTS

Tell a non-cyclist you ride a bike and they assume you must be fit, sustainable, resourceful and self-reliant.

THE CYCLE OF LIFE

Like a retro music artist rediscovered after decades out of fashion, cycling is suddenly cool again.

From hip ad campaigns to mundane council leaflets, we're bombarded with images of happy people on bikes. Briefcase-toting commuters eager to get to work; carefree families bonding on a rail trail (*see* 'Glossary', page 119); racing pelotons cresting a mountain pass; flowing-haired young women in summer frocks with a puppy in their front basket...

The reality is often different: mending your second puncture on a windy November night on the bypass; being cut up repeatedly by the same bus; getting thrown off a train because your reserved bike space is blocked by a hen party's airline baggage.

Cyclists know this. Tell them you ride a bike and they will welcome you as a fellow chosen one – a member of the special people – who knows about quality of life, and who won't harangue them about jumping red lights, or cycling on pavements, or 'road tax'. But non-cyclists don't know this. Tell them you ride a bike and they assume you must be fit, sustainable, resourceful and self-reliant.

They're instantly on the defensive, burbling excuses about needing their car because they live so far away. And they have to live so far away because nowhere else has parking. They know they should use their bike but it has a flat tyre. And there's a hill.

With all those media images in mind, they're envious of, and a little intimidated by, the vibrant, sociable and healthy lifestyle they presume you must have.

Riding a bike is great. It saves temper, time and money. You glide past traffic queues, arrive early feeling fit, and get 300 miles per gallon of coffee. It puts you in direct control of your resources.

Bluffing about it is even better, because it puts you in control of other people. And that's what being a bluffer is all about.

This short guide sets out to conduct you through the main danger zones encountered in discussions about cycling, and to equip you with a vocabulary and evasive technique that will minimise the risk of being rumbled as a bluffer. It will give you a few easy-to-learn hints and techniques that might even allow you to be accepted as a cyclist of rare knowledge and experience. But it will do more. It will give you the tools to impress legions of marvelling listeners with your wisdom and insight – without anyone discovering that until you read it you probably didn't know the difference between a velocipede and a centipede.

BIKE MYTHS
AND MILESTONES

No one country, let alone one person, invented the bike, which evolved from the collective efforts of many people. But that hasn't stopped various people claiming otherwise through bicycle creation myths.

As with regular history, the way to sound knowledgeable is to wait for people to make some assertion. Then, you rebut what they've said as commonly held myth, very misleading, or, at the very least, 'I think you'll find it's not as simple as it looks' (a good fallback position that can be used for pretty much everything, except perhaps daytime TV).

The most surprising thing about bikes is how early all the technology familiar on modern machines was in place. The Rover safety bicycle of 1885 looks very much like a modern town bike (it even had mudguards – though it would handle rather differently, as you'd soon find out when trying to brake going downhill).

MYTH:

DA VINCI DESIGNED A BICYCLE

In Leonardo da Vinci's notebook *Codex Atlanticus*, there's a drawing resembling a nineteenth-century 'velocipede' with the addition of a startlingly prescient chain and pedals. It's sometimes credited to Leonardo's pupil Gian Giacomo Caprotti, circa 1493, but overwhelming scholarly opinion now is that it's a forgery. Profess amazement that so many were taken in by a patently anachronistic fake: 'Didn't the writing on the frame, "RALEIGH – MADE IN NOTTINGHAM", give it away?' (Ideally, the other person will refer to 'da Vinci', which you can correct to 'Leonardo' – surnames hadn't yet caught on in fifteenth-century rural Italy. Calling him 'da Vinci', you can say, is like referring to John of Gaunt as 'Mr of Gaunt'.)

MYTH:

STOKE POGES CHURCH HAS A SEVENTEENTH-CENTURY BICYCLE WINDOW

St Giles' Church in Stoke Poges, Buckinghamshire, has a stained glass window dating from 1643 which shows an angel apparently riding a prototype 'hobbyhorse' (*see* opposite). In fact, it's only a one-wheeled contraption of a sort that cherubim, seraphim and angelim are often shown sitting on in stained glass windowim; a curve at the back, largely hidden by a strut, misleads the modern eye into thinking there's a back wheel somewhere.

That said, the angel is stark naked and blowing a trumpet, which is spookily predictive of the annual fleshfest that is the World Naked Bike Ride.

MILESTONE:

DRAIS INVENTED THE HOBBYHORSE

The first practical two-wheeled personal transport mode. Between 1817 and 1819, the *laufmaschine*, or velocipede, or *draisine*, or *draisienne*, developed by Baron Karl von Drais of Germany, was all the rage. Though pedal-less – riders used their feet to scoot along – it established several things we now think of as essential to the bicycle: two in-line wheels, the front being steerable; the rider sitting on a platform in between the wheels; and most important, pavement cycling, which became such a menace to pedestrians that it led to the first laws banishing bicycles from footways in 1835. It was around the time of Drais's invention that the word velocipede really caught on as a generic term for describing a human-powered land vehicle with two wheels.

If someone calls Drais's version a hobbyhorse, furrow your brow and point out that this particular term came in when Denis Johnson, a London coachmaker, tweaked the draisienne, calling it a 'pedestrian curricle', though the public preferred 'hobbyhorse' or 'dandyhorse'. This established another bicycle essential: a eurobabel where every language has a different word for each cycling term.

On 12 June 1817, Drais took the very first bike ride in the world. He covered eight miles from Mannheim in just under an hour. Presumably the first instance of a cab driver shouting that the cyclist should pay road tax happened the same day.

Sadly, the sheer discomfort of Drais's machine meant that most people bought it in a flush of enthusiasm, rode it a couple of times, then – with sore behinds and aching legs – chucked it to the back of the shed. Another bicycle essential established.

MYTH:

KIRKPATRICK MACMILLAN INVENTED THE FIRST PEDAL BICYCLE

In 1839, a Dumfries smithy called Kirkpatrick Macmillan built the first pedal-cranked two-wheel machine, or so the tale goes. He was supposedly fined five shillings for colliding with a pedestrian in a very painful place – the Gorbals. However, there's no evidence. The legend arose from a dubious letter sent decades later to a newspaper by his nephew claiming the whole thing, citing a vague old newspaper report (which doesn't mention Macmillan) as evidence. Modern opinion, including yours, is that the story is a load of cobblers.

MILESTONE:

PEOPLE START RIDING BONESHAKERS

From the 1820s to the 1850s, huge, unwieldy machines with three or four wheels appeared (mention Willard Sawyer of Dover). Most were driven by cranks, although some were relatively sane. Propelled by pedals, treadles and paddles, they never really took off. Except down steep slopes.

But then, in the 1860s, a Frenchman had the bright idea of adding pedals to the front wheel of the draisienne, and the first popular pedallable bicycle was born. It was either Pierre Lallement or his rival Pierre Michaux; whichever people suggest, insist it was the other. Mass-produced and relatively cheap, it sparked a brief velocipede craze in France, England and the USA, with races, magazines and rants in the popular press about these dangerous imbeciles on velocipedes. The iron-banded wooden wheels gave a jarring ride – hence the nickname 'boneshakers'. You can take issue with anyone using the term, though, insisting that in Paris, on nice, smooth 'macadamised' roads introduced in the centre, and on the many velocipede rinks which sprung up, it was perfectly comfortable.

MISLEADING MILESTONE:

PEOPLE RODE 'PENNY-FARTHINGS'

From the 1860s to the mid-1880s, the standard bike – especially in England – was the 'penny-farthing'. This was a sort of logical extension of a boneshaker, with the front wheel massively enlarged to make speeds above crawling pace possible, and to better cope with bumpy roads. Except that, at the time, it was called a 'high-wheeler' or 'high bicycle', and later, in retrospect, an 'ordinary'. So, feel free to rubbish anyone who tries to call it a 'penny-farthing'. The father of the high bicycle was either James Starley of England, or Eugene Meyer of France – again, whichever people put forward, insist the other was the true pioneer.

High-wheelers were difficult to ride and dangerous, and almost exclusively the preserve of daring young men, one of whom – Thomas Stevens – was the first to cycle around the world, in 1884–1886. He took little luggage apart from a raincoat that doubled as a tent, and a gun. (He'd clearly cycled in London.) Many others only got as far as the first downhill before being thrown over the handlebars, 'coming a cropper', and breaking their wrists in the fall.

Talk knowledgeably about the technical challenges – the unreliable spoon-shaped brakes pressing down on the solid rubber tyre, the difficulty of pedalling the wheel while turning it, the mounting and dismounting – as if you had personal experience ('I had a go once' – in other words, you were politely asked not to touch one in Hull's transport museum).

MILESTONE:

STARLEY INVENTED THE MODERN-PATTERN SAFETY BICYCLE

High bicycles with smaller, geared wheels, and a back-to-front design (with the 'farthing' at the front) were actually called 'safeties'. But the term quickly became applied to the revolutionary new shape of the 1880s. A rush of new technology between about 1885 and 1891 established the familiar modern bicycle: pedals driving the rear wheel via a chain and alterable gears; steerable front wheel of the same size; diamond frame; sprung saddle…and punctures.

Gene pools diversified as suitors were no longer confined to a walking radius (or a running radius when they got caught).

The first modern bicycle was indeed the landmark 1885 Rover, designed by John Kemp Starley (nephew of James). Racing, touring and utility cycling boomed in England,

France and the rest of Europe, as the middle classes could now afford to ride in comfort and safety. A bike felt about as expensive as a car would today, usually bought on credit, and the idea of 'this year's model' was soon established.

Gene pools diversified as suitors were no longer confined to a walking radius (or a running radius when they got caught). Women, discarded their skirts in favour of 'rational dress', such as the more practical bloomers (named after Amelia Bloomer, the American social reformer who had started the long ride to emancipation). In 1895, Annie Londonderry became the first woman to ride around the world, which can lead you neatly into talk of feminism if you need to change the subject, or just annoy someone.

MYTH:

JOHN BOYD DUNLOP INVENTED THE PNEUMATIC TYRE

The Scottish vet working in Belfast certainly patented the inflatable tyre, and mass production by his Dunlop company revolutionised cycling. The tyres made it far more comfortable and gave cyclists the chance to enjoy the view for three hours while they repaired punctures (which initially involved ungluing the tyre from the rim). However, he had unwittingly reinvented what had already been patented for horse-drawn carriages, making his patent worthless; deft legal work with modified designs managed to save his business though. Contrarians can claim Frenchman Édouard Michelin as the real cycle-rubberwear pioneer, with his 1891 patent for the more convenient detachable inner tube.

MYTH:

ROADS WERE BUILT FOR CARS IN THE EARLY 1900S

Cars began to sweep bicycles aside, almost literally, from the early 1900s, and the great cycling boom faded: first in the USA, then, in the second half of the century, in Europe. But it's quite wrong to associate better roads with cars: surfaces had already started being tarmacked and improved, largely due to pressure from cycle campaigners.

MYTH:

THE TWENTIETH CENTURY HAD ALL THE TECHNOLOGICAL INNOVATIONS

Technology through the twentieth century grew by evolution rather than revolution; you can correctly claim that all 'modern' advances, including derailleur gears, aluminium frames, disc wheels, anatomical saddles, clipless pedals, suspension and folding bikes, in fact originated during the reign of Queen Victoria (who owned a Starley Royal Salvo tricycle, a whirling iron monster – though she never actually rode it).

MISLEADING MILESTONE:

MOUNTAIN BIKING WAS INVENTED IN THE LATE TWENTIETH CENTURY

Mountain bikes were first mass-produced in 1981, following a 1970s downhilling craze in Orange County, California, and have become the standard pattern leisure bicycle. But this is nothing new – people have been falling off head-first into mud in hurtling descents since high-wheeler days. Describe mountain biking as marketing, rather than technological, progress. Or, if you don't understand why a bike in a rainy town centre has no mudguards, regress.

MYTH:

HG WELLS AND OTHER QUOTES

Challenge anyone who cites a juicy quote about cycling to provide a source that isn't merely someone's blog, or a webpage anthology. Take the much-pasted one attributed to HG Wells, for instance: 'When I see an adult on a bicycle, I do not despair for the future of the human race'. The trouble is, no one has ever found a source for it. Wells did, however, say 'Cycle tracks will abound in Utopia' (*A Modern Utopia*).

MYTH:

CYCLISTS SHOULD PAY ROAD TAX

In the early twenty-first century, questions of how cyclists and motor vehicles should share resources have become major agenda items. Again, this is nothing new – 'scorchers', or reckless cyclists, were already the subject of endless diatribes in newspaper letters pages 120 years earlier.

Rebuttals to the road-tax myth are detailed on page 52. In practice, you'll only get halfway through the first one before most cyclist-baiters get bored and go away. Which is probably what you wanted all along.

MYTH:

THE TOUR DE FRANCE
HAS THE MOST AND BIGGEST MOUNTAINS

The routes of the Giro d'Italia and Spain's Vuelta are tougher and have more climbs with a height gain of over 2,000 metres than France. You can risk quoting the world's most infamous cyclist if you feel brave: Lance Armstrong says Mortirolo on the Giro is the toughest climb he's ever done – over 10% gradient. But then it's amazing what a transfusion of freshly-oxygenated blood can do for your stamina.

MYTH:

ALPE D'HUEZ IS THE TOUGHEST CLIMB ON
THE TOUR DE FRANCE

The climb's 'beyond category' status comes because it usually falls at the end of a stage, when riders are knackered. In steepness and length, Alpe d'Huez is a mere 7.5% for nine miles, making it what would normally be a humdrum Category 1 climb.

Imply that you know the Tour's classic climbs (Galibier, Mont Ventoux, Iseran, etc.; if you run out of names, use nineteenth-century authors or car manufacturers) from experience, perhaps having cycled in France, and therefore having seen them first-hand, on postcards.

CYCLING TRIBES

As a bluffer, you should know your tribes. Cyclists are not one big happy family, but a diverse and separate bunch with different, sometimes rival, attributes. Select which of the following 15 you want to appear to belong to. Obviously this depends on who you're trying to impress.

ECO-WARRIOR

Believes The world is dying and it's your fault. You should boycott planes, cars, supermarkets, fast-food chains, major brands and profitable businesses, except for the ones they use. Everyone should cycle because it's sustainable, like in countries like, um, Africa.

Spiritual home Glastonbury, Wales, tent, friend's floor.

Wears Shabby jeans or skirt. Slogan T-shirt. Facial piercings. No helmet; anyway, won't fit over the dreadlocks.

Rides Tatty old town bike with broken mudguards, fluffy saddle cover and stickers promoting erstwhile worthy causes.

CAMPAIGNER

Believes Buses, taxis, councils, police, media, world, all part of motoring-lobby conspiracy. Cycle facilities (or the lack of them) are good for one thing only – exposing on their blog. Everyone should cycle so they can film bad driving and post the footage on YouTube.

Spiritual home Outside city-centre shops, photographing lack of cycle parking.

Wears Helmetcam, high-visibility jacket, camera, notebook, iPhone permanently running 'pothole complaints' app.

Rides Heavily accessorised town bike: mirror, computer, twin-set lights, GPS, factory-strength horn.

COURIER

Believes Life is for living, preferably on the edge, such as the pavement's. Couriering is just a stopgap to pay for parties, bikes, music, shared flat, until a more meaningful job comes along, such as…er…

Spiritual home City of London main road, squeezing between railings and bus to jump the lights.

Wears Raggy casuals, radical tattoos, extreme hairstyle, stretched lobes. Sculpted beard (men only). Shoulder bag toting urgent corporate delivery: meaningless promo DVD, meaningless press release, meaningless event invite, etc.

Rides Single-speed (for agility) narrow-handlebar (for squeezing between lines of traffic) minimalist (for lightness and speed) bike with anvil-sized maximum-security lock dangling on handlebars (for threatening taxi drivers who cut them up).

MAMIL (MIDDLE-AGED MAN IN LYCRA)

Believes It's never too late. Panting up the stairs last year, but suddenly got into cycling when the big Four-O came along. Has never felt better: new friends, new lease of life. Shame wife doesn't get it.

Spiritual home Provincial suburb, reading triathlon magazine in bed.

Wears Rainforest toad-coloured polyester cycling top. Helmet, especially when sat in pub beer garden. Lycra tights, whose elasticity is essential for main evening activity – accommodating tea-room cake on the club run.

Rides £2,000 carbon-fibre road bike that topped the 'budget' comparative review in last month's *Cycling Plus* magazine. Spends more time talking about it than riding it.

POETIC SOUL

Believes World moves too fast – that is, anything faster than bicycle pace. Wonders how people rushing to work in cars or trains have time to write their novel. Likes social aspect of cycling – can go to pub to escape family and read book in peace. If only more people spent time cycling instead of making and selling things, world economy wouldn't be in meltdown.

Spiritual home Reading Larkin in remote village graveyard.

Wears Trad, fogeyish garb: raincoat, hat, scarf, tweed jacket, slacks, brogues, etc.

Rides 1950s women's Raleigh three-speed. Chainguard. Bell. Saddlebag containing sandwich, TS Eliot book, *The Guardian* crossword.

WEEKEND MTBER (MOUNTAIN BIKER)

Believes Leisure time precious, so spends hours on motorway driving to remote forest to enjoy it. Everyone should cycle, so long as they have an SUV with bike carrier in order to do it.

Spiritual home Post-ride pub with mates near forest trails such as Coed-y-Brenin or Dalby Forest. Can't drink, though, as driving.

Wears Waterproof jacket with vertical stripe of ingrained mud up back. Lycra. Forehead scar from last year's face plant (*see* 'Glossary', page 118), with pride. Safety first: helmet always, because this means you can take more risks.

Rides Mid-range full-suspension mountain bike which spends more time on roof rack than on ground.

Not sure of make because no one's ever seen the frame through the mud.

COMMUTER

Believes Everyone should cycle to work as it's the fastest, most reliable way, and makes for more productive employees – and 20-minute shower on arrival is on company time.

Spiritual home At desk, after shower, feeling fit and alert, ready to switch on PC and get to work browsing cycling feeds on Twitter.

Wears Insect-eye sunglasses, Lycra, dazzling yellow high-visibility jacket even on a bright summer morning – distracts from red light just jumped. Small backpack stuffed with towel, toiletries, smart trousers – and 10 minutes to iron them is on company time.

Rides Fast road bike, or top-end folder, cut-price through cycle-to-work scheme. Bought after thorough research of best-buy reviews on money-saving website one afternoon at work.

RACER

Believes No pain, no train, no gain. The Tour de France is the ultimate physical challenge – look at Coppi, Anquetil, Hinault, Indurain, Merckx – no, they're riders, not climbs; you're thinking of Galibier, Tourmalet, Alpe d'Huez – look at Tom Simpson, there's a role model, died on Mont Ventoux after an overdose – no, not wine – look, are you taking this seriously?

Spiritual home Leading peloton up viciously steep hill, sucking energy gel, or back home examining computer's heart-monitor profile of ride.

Wears Grimace. Otherwise, same as MAMIL.

Rides As Lance's (him again) autobiography said, it's not about the bike. But just in case it is, it's a £5,000 carbon-fibre Pinarello.

TOURER

Believes In not being cooped up in a car or coach's metal cage in order to genuinely interact with people, places, sunstroke, midges, etc. Can experience the fresh air, especially headwind. Can go as you please: nothing can stop you, except trains and buses refusing to take the bike; rain; outdated maps that fail to show this is now a motorway; and mechanical failure on Saturday night 30 miles from the next town. It's called freedom. Everyone should travel this way.

Spiritual home Village bus stop, sheltering from rain with sandwich and water bottle, trying to get mobile reception to book a B&B.

Wears T-shirt, shorts, shades.

Rides Heavily loaded touring bike: bulging front and rear panniers with drying clothes draped over tent, sleeping mat and various supermarket plastic bags strapped to rack; three water bottles, one full of last night's leftover red wine; bar bag with valuables such as passport, camera, cake.

GEEK

Believes In rationalism and science – such as the ideal number of bikes being determined by the formula $n+1$, where n is the number of bikes currently owned.

Spiritual home Their lock-up garage, tinkering with a derelict 1980s Dawes Galaxy rescued from a skip for restoration; or on eBay, bidding for that 1940s dynamo set.

Wears Yesterday's clothes; slightly unnerving smile; their partner's patience thin.

Rides Recumbent. Or 1960s shopper. Or Dursley Pedersen*. Or electric bike. Or unicycle.

* Eccentric 1920s design resembling wheeled trellis with hammock saddle. Must-have for bike geeks.

CHARITY RIDER

Believes Cycling is dangerous and difficult, so can only be undertaken in organised groups once a year. Also painful, so friends should pay you to withstand it. But at least you can raise lots of money to subsidise poor people, such as those who run the charity rides. And you have a holiday that only costs a bit more than if you did it by bus and train.

Spiritual home Justgiving.com donation page with beaming location photo captioned 'Finished at last!! Now can put bike back in garage for another year!!!!!'.

Wears T-shirt with charity logo; padded shorts; their friends' resistance down with relentless 'sponsor-me-I-must-be-mad' email campaign.

Rides What do you mean, what sort of bike? You know, a pushbike. With wheels and stuff. The one in the garage.

OVERPROTECTIVE FAMILY

Believes The confidence and independence that comes with road cycling helps children prepare for the adult world. But not yet, obviously; they can't cycle to school – they have to be driven there because it's too dangerous, thanks to all the traffic doing the school run. Instead they must be chaperoned on a car-free rail trail, or closed-road annual organised event, corporately sponsored, where in a safe environment they can get a taste of confidence-building life skills, such as how to run PR events and media campaigns.

Spiritual home Local park, making sure children don't fall off onto the grass, because they might be allergic to chlorophyll.

Wears Helmets, probably on backwards. Sunblock and waterproofs. Sunglasses and reflective clothing.

Rides 'Tagalong' for the kids (one-wheel trailer bike that fits on parent's seatpost). Parents' bikes have tall plastic flags. Picnic basket with gluten- and nut-free organic lunch, herbal tea, soya milk, etc.

UTILITY CYCLIST

Believes Who needs a car for shopping and A-to-B travel? We should be like the Netherlands, where bike-friendly centres mean everyone cycles – rich, poor, old, young, criminals, terrorists, etc. Britain's towns would be much more pleasant places if all towns had separated cycle lanes, like delightful Stevenage or Milton Keynes. Conservative politicians tend to be members of this tribe; also often seen being trailed by a black gas guzzler bearing vital documents of state.

Spiritual home The Netherlands. Failing that, Cambridge. Failing that, any town that's flat, scenery-free and windy. Westminster is quite popular.

Wears Everyday clothes for cycling – as you can tell by the oil stains and holes in the trousers. Definitely no helmet – panniers full of shopping serve as buffers in unlikely event of accident doing 5mph between supermarket and post office.

Rides Battered but sturdy town bike, possibly with trailer, creaking under weight of weekly shop, bag of cement, hatstand, child, etc.

RETIREMENT CLUB-RUNNER

Believes What better way to spend your 'third age' than cycling out to the countryside with pals from the club? And no chance of meeting rowdy youths – they're too podgy to keep up.

Spiritual home Long, narrow country lane, 50 miles from their suburban home.

Wears Same gear as MAMIL, only less new-looking. Happy smile. Lycra longs out, regularly.

Rides Dawes Super Galaxy that's as old as their wedding anniversary.

BEST SORT OF CYCLIST

Believes Pretty much what you think.

Spiritual home Same sort of place where you're most comfortable.

Wears Sometimes very similar to what you're wearing now.

Rides As it happens, almost exactly the same bike as you.

Note: This list does not include those whose bikes never go near a road, such as BMX or track cycling. These are NPBs – not proper bikes. After all, if you've never been cut up by a bus, you're not exactly a real cyclist.

BUYING A BIKE

The smartest bike-buying option is second-hand. Decent bikes retain their value and decades-old quality machines can easily be upgraded with new components. So you can suggest you got an incredible bargain on, say, eBay (in practice, unlikely: you'll end up paying over the odds in the deadline frenzy for something unseen and pick-up only in Exeter or Aberdeen) or Gumtree (in practice, unlikely: why was that seller hazy about the bike's provenance, only willing to give a mobile number, and advertising 15 other bikes?) or at a police auction (in practice, scrap metal).

Most probably though you'll be buying new. Disparage anyone who buys online: insist you must try out a bike before you commit to it. Like a lover. An internet bike in a box is like getting engaged by Skype to a mail-order spouse from Albania.

Supermarkets are also out: a bike that costs the same as a bottle of birthday champagne will last about as long. Their shopping trolleys would give you a more comfortable, more steerable ride.

Which leaves you with the retail chains (in other words, Evans and Halfords) or independent local bike shops. There's little difference in price, but the chains have better car parking. That suits the sort of buyer whose bike will do more miles in the rear of the hatchback than on the rail trail.

Staff at indie shops are generally more knowledgeable, and not on a gap year saving up for a snowboarding trip. Independents are the ones to approve of, in case you're wondering which way to exaggerate a story. Refer to the owner by first name to imply familiarity with expertise ('Andy from Cycle Heaven was telling me...').

There are two main types of bike: ones people want, and ones they actually need.

Of course, you'd never buy this season's expensive model: you bought last season's model at a silly clearance price.

Hint that you bought any new bike through the cycle-to-work scheme. Firms registered with the scheme let their employees hire-purchase a bike in a tax-efficient way (at effectively half price) with a small monthly deduction from their pay slips. Perhaps you exploited some loophole to make it even cheaper. (Unless the other person says they bought their bike this way, in which case breathe in sharply and say that recent changes have made it less lucrative. Warn of tax-investigation implications if they're found to have used it outside work; hire-purchase means the bike is the company's not yours, etc.)

TYPES OF BIKE

There are two main types of bike: ones people want, and ones they actually need.

What most people want is a cheap mountain bike with 27 gears, tractor tyres, full suspension, no mudguards, disc brakes, and a big soft saddle. But their imagined countryside hill climbs and technical descents won't happen. Instead they'll do one flat bank holiday rail trail, before the bike goes in the shed for the winter.

What most people actually need is a middlingly expensive town bike with medium tyres, seven or so gears (easily enough for everything except rugged off-road and racing), no suspension (costly to maintain), proper mudguards (essential in towns), normal brakes and a small firm saddle (less of a pain in the backside).

But shops sell what people will buy, not what they need, so you'll only see a couple of such things in the showroom, shuffled over into the corner at a discount. Otherwise the shop will be full of road and mountain bikes.

You can think of bikes on a scale of riding position, from meerkat-upright (town bikes) to wiping-nose-on-handlebars (racers). Similarly, handlebars go from wheelbarrow-style (town bikes), through flat bars (hybrids and mountain bikes) to deer-antler drops (tourers and racers) to Superman-splayed-forward-arm racks (triathlon).

Here's a rundown of them, from most common to rarest, and a guide to how to work out what type the purchaser should have bought instead. Imply you used to have one of those, before you realised what a waste of money it was, and flogged it to a willing mug online.

Note that some types of bike cross over into one another, especially when one of them ignores a red light at a junction.

HYBRID

The 'generic bike': basically a mountain bike, but less rugged.

Advantages Usable for city streets, light off-road towpaths or rail trails; robust enough to stand being crammed into back of garage for 360 days of the year.

Disadvantages Only three of the 27 gears ever get used, meaning expensive replacement of whole kit when those three wear out. Lack of mudguards turns bike into urban muck-spreader in the wet. Lack of rack means riders carry luggage in rucksack on back, which is uncomfortable and sweaty – so rather uncomfortable for co-workers or pub-seat neighbours too.

What they should have bought instead Town bike ('Where exactly are the mountains in your town centre?').

MOUNTAIN BIKE (MTB)

Intended for rough hill climbs and descents. Flat handlebars, suspension probably rear and possibly front, strong brakes, 20-odd gears, big fat tyres of 26 inches (too small) or 29 (too big), and car-style Schrader valves, bare-bones appearance: no mudguards or frills, even cheap frills.

Advantages Low gears for uphill; rugged enough to cope with very rough stony tracks, and being thrown into the boot of a car or the back of an ambulance.

Disadvantages Tiring and inefficient to ride on road and can't carry luggage, so only good for off-road day circuits involving long car or train journeys.

What they should have bought instead Next year's model with much better spec; or last year's model with similar spec but much cheaper.

BICYCLE-SHAPED OBJECT (BSO)

Imitation mountain bike sold dirt-cheap online or in supermarkets. Comes ready for self-assembly in box. Box probably more robust and better ride.

Advantages Mechanically-minded owner can make it into acceptable bike by replacing a few parts, such as brakes, saddle, chain, gears, wheels, handlebars, mudguards and frame.

Disadvantages Classic mistake is to fit front forks the wrong way round, making bike very uncomfortable and possibly dangerous to ride. Next mistake is to fit forks the right way round, also making bike very uncomfortable and possibly dangerous to ride. Every part is such poor quality that it's just not solid. Especially the back wheel.

What they should have bought instead A bike.

ROAD BIKE
Built for speed and racing on smooth tarmac. 700C wheels (700mm, thanks to French not US origin) and Presta valves with screwable collar. Razor-blade saddle, possibly carbon-fibre frame. Flashily coloured, skeletal and lightweight, and virtually silent, like its rider.

Advantages Cutting-edge technology, especially when you fall onto it on a 50mph downhill. Light as a feather – handy when the thin tyres puncture and, not carrying tools, you have to carry it back to the car.

Disadvantages Desirable, hence stealable, but strong-enough lock weighs more than bike, defeating point; hence can never park it. Narrow tyres mean discomfort on anything but very smooth roads, though this does mask the pain of climbing Hardknott Pass non-stop.

What they should have bought instead Apparently identical model but half a pound lighter and a thousand pounds more expensive ('if it makes just 0.1% difference over the course of a race…[raise eyebrows, open palms]').

FOLDING BIKE

Usually small-wheel jobs for rail commuters, but also come in mountain-bike, road-bike, even electric-bike versions. Seem to defy some instinctive law of transport resources: you can ride to Sydney on one, but it decants into a shopping bag. Or even smaller areas, such as bicycle spaces on trains.

Advantages Can sleep, compacted catlike, in the cupboard under the stairs, instead of attacking people's shins in the hallway. Can nestle under restaurant and pub tables so you don't have to lock them to the NO CYCLES HERE sign outside. Can slip into car boots without struggle, unlike kidnap victims. Depreciate little, so if you really do get stuck, you can sell it and get a taxi. They delight small children, as they watch you trying in vain to unfold it. (Hint for Bromptons: raise saddle first.)

Disadvantages Cheap ones are awful, good ones (Bromptons) are expensive. Ride is never as comfy as normal bike.

What they should have bought instead One less quickly or compactly folded but with better ride quality (if they cycle more than say two miles between train and work); or vice-versa (if less than two miles). But a more expensive one, either way.

TOWN BIKE (AKA DUTCH BIKE)

Tall, sturdy, upright, probably Dutch – that's the sort of rider using this one. In Britain, more likely in bike-promo ads, when ridden by long-haired young woman in frock, than on street, when ridden by grey-haired old man in cloth cap. Step-through frame suits both. Few gears, none high: takes so long to build up momentum from lights, no point.

Advantages Great for muscle development as you haul it over kerbs or up stairs. Great for shopping and café-hopping, hence bad for waistline. Currently retro-chic. Chainguard, mudguards, rack, bell, basket, pump, kickstand – so high scrap/parts value when fashion cycle makes it uncool again. Relatively undesirable to thieves without forklift.

Disadvantages Good ones surprisingly expensive – but fantastic value per hundredweight.

What they should have bought instead A folder would be just as handy around town, but extend possibilities of using train, bus, etc.; and easier to hide under stairs when neglected. If comfort is issue, iron bed on casters would offer similar experience for less money.

TOURING BIKE

Built for distance in comfort with big loads – the estate car of bikes. Drop handlebars enable rider to duck under inevitable all-day headwinds. Racks and panniers at rear, possibly front too, crammed with round-the-world luggage essentials (HD video, smartphone, laptop for blogging, etc.) despite only going to Wetherspoon's.

Advantages Sturdy frame and tyres sufficient to cope with rough surfaces: farm tracks, canal towpaths, even some London roads. Excellent for shopping: can carry enough to double value of bike.

Disadvantages Niche market, so pricey and hard to find. Good ones last forever, so no excuse to upgrade to this year's shiny new model.

What they should have bought instead Can try telling them 'trekking bike' (vague term for tourer-hybrid) but they won't listen, as they'll be too busy showing you the pics from their last tour.

E-BIKES

Usually hybrids, but can be any other sort, with added electric motor that only boosts your pedalling – it won't work solely by itself. Next year is when e-bikes will go mainstream, and always is.

Advantages Turns uphills into plains, headwinds into refreshing breezes, gravel into smooth tarmac. Huge fun to ride. Excellent for leisure touring. Boon for disabled, infirm or elderly riders. Health benefits, such as developing biceps when trying to lift them.

Disadvantages Good ones (reliable motor, long-life battery pack) very expensive. Very heavy, as you find when battery runs out before that big hill. Perceptions of 'cheating', in fact usually envy.

What they should have bought instead More expensive one with longer range, better engineering and crank-, not hub-, motor. Or less expensive one so they could actually afford the holiday it was bought for.

EXOTIC BIKES

Recumbents Armchair with wheels; favourite with geeks, who customise their comfy space lavishly – handlebar hi-fi, multi-angle video cameras, drinks cabinet, etc. Fast on the flat, but hard up hills. Near invisible in traffic but very prominent on YouTube.

Tandem Two-person bike. Not allowed on trains; hard to find parking spaces. Faster in theory because of less wind resistance, but slower in practice because person behind (stoker) never pulls their weight – at least so person in front (captain) believes. Hence can threaten a relationship. Goes downhill fast. So does tandem.

Fixie Minimalist style statement for zippy urban chic: zero gears, zero freewheel, zero lights. Probably ancient-but-quality frame resprayed, with zero added to price.

Tricycle Curiously tiring and odd to steer. Offers stability advantages at its most efficient speed – stationary.

Hand cycle Tremendously enabling transport for many with mobility problems – until they get to the barriers at that council cycle track.

Unicycles, BMX, track bikes Don't even think about trying to bluff on anything that doesn't have brakes; never mind attempt to ride them.

SELECTING THE RIGHT BIKE

Talk confidently about the bike-fitting process. Everyone recognises that a bike must be fitted, like a bespoke suit, to the exact body shape of the rider – arm length, leg length and so on. And as nobody apart from expert bike builders knows the details, you can say pretty much what you like and it'll impress most people. Talk vaguely about measuring 'standover height' (how high a crossbar you can take without extending your vocal range) by involved processes such as leaning against a wall and getting a friend to put a book between your legs as high as it will go, comfortably. It won't help you determine the right frame size much, but it's a fun way to spend an afternoon, especially with an imaginative choice of book.

Traditional guidelines relating frame size to leg length are only of general help now, thanks to small mountain bike frames, so you can divert the topic to saddles, which everyone can relate to.

Everyone will think they understand your main points about saddles:

1. Inexpert cyclists always have their saddle too low. (The leg should almost be straight with the pedal at the bottom.)

2. They wrongly believe a big soft saddle is more comfy. (Small firm ones are better.)

3. Women need different saddle shapes to men.

Men benefit from a hollow so their prostate doesn't get squashed – you can move the conversation away here to entertaining anecdotes about medical examinations. Dismiss any talk of saddles causing impotence though; it was 'one rogue study from the USA' concerning only 'triathletes on drugs', and imply that 'other studies have suggested cyclists are actually more fertile than non-cyclists'. That's not true, but most people will happily believe it.

Women don't benefit from a hollow, but do need wider saddles as their sit bones are wider apart than men's. A woman using a man's saddle will find it uncomfortable, and according to your sexual politics, you can blame the man who sold it to her (for being ignorant) or the woman who bought it (for being ignorant).

BITS AND BOLTS

Cycling requires little in the way of equipment. Lycra and lemon-curd tops, for instance, are useful for showing off that you've cycled to that remote village pub, but are not for real, everyday cyclists. The most useful items to have, in order of priority, are:

1. BIKE LIGHTS

Bike lights are essential. Far removed from the battery-eating monsters of the pre-internet age, modern LED models can slip in your pocket and last all winter on one set of batteries. They also serve as makeshift torches for scenarios where illumination is bad – reading the menu in tapas bars, for example, or walking along an off-road bike path.

Cheap ones, from the pound shop, for instance, are the reality-show celebs of bike equipment: flashy, dim, and soon fall to pieces. But they're useful to have in your pannier to give 'generously' to cyclists you meet whose pub overstay means they are about to risk cycling home in the dark unlit. The exchange rate for a pound shop pair of lights is three drinks – a handsome return.

You can spook anyone proud of their gimmicky lights – wind-up rechargeables for instance – by querying if they are BS6102/3 compliant. If not, they're illegal by themselves: your bike must be lit with BS-compliant stuff at night and you can be stopped and fined if not. However, as you can point out if someone complains about your lack of lights, hard evidence that poorly-lit bikes are more likely to be involved in accidents is actually hard to find.

You can also point out that sometimes, cycling on a deserted road or cycle track at night, you're safer not using lights: they contract your pupils, making your vision worse outside the tiny pool of white light in front of you. Whether or not you do, saying so makes you sound confident and experienced – the sort of person who cycles under romantically moonlit circumstances.

2. PUMP ADAPTOR

A pump adaptor is a tiny metal ring which converts between the two types of inner-tube valve – Presta (racing bikes) and Schrader (mountain bikes, the same as a car tyre's). Always carry one. They cost a few pence but are worth their weight in gold, because on every sunny-day leisure cycle track there's someone standing bewildered by their upturned bike, with a flat tyre of one sort and a pump of the other.

Being able to rescue them from their format incompatibility – especially if they're attractive and of your preferred gender – could make the adaptor the best investment you've ever made. It suggests you're a rugged, capable, go-anywhere sort who can service a boiler or strangle a croc with your bare hands, when all you've done is keep a 50p piece of brass in your toolkit.

As for pumps themselves, free public ones are installed in several London streets (the first was outside the Three Stags pub in Kennington) – but otherwise the must-have is a track pump, one of those stirrup things that bike shops grumpily lend passing cyclists who then don't spend any money.

3. BIKE HIRE

You don't actually need to own a bike to bluff confidently about cycling, thanks to an increasing number of hire options. Others' doubts over your experience of e-bikes, top-end frames, folding tandem mountain bikes etc., can be rebutted by claiming you once hired such a bike.

Foreign touring Two options here. Either you hired a five-grand carbon-fibre Cannondale in Spain for a 'training week with the guys/girls' for 100 euros, or a clanky old town bike to explore some developing-country town 'where the tourists never go' for 25p.

UK leisure rides Most popular trails offer hire bikes – convenient but expensive, especially e-bikes. Always worth implying you got some sort of special discount or deal.

City bikes Many British towns have local schemes allowing you to sign up and rent a bike cheaply for 30-90 minutes, taking from one docking station and returning to another – a concept pioneered by Paris's Vélib. The UK's schemes come and go though, and none are on the vast scale of London's 'Boris bikes'. Nicknamed after the mayor who happened to be in office on their introduction in 2010, Boris Johnson, they're currently sponsored by Santander. Either you think they're flexible and fun, the best way to get around the capital, and have transformed the capital's leisure biking culture; or they're an expensive vanity scheme that don't relieve congestion and only cast wobbly tourists on to busy streets.

Dockless bike hire Pioneered in the Far East by companies such as Ofo and Mobike, such app-based schemes dispense with docking stations, and their brightly coloured bikes are appearing all over many big British towns, usually parked on footpaths. Hirers use the app to find the nearest bike where another user left it, and leave it anywhere after their ride. The bottom of a canal, or up a tree, for instance.

If challenged as to why you
don't have a bike, say it was stolen –
everyone will believe that.

---

4. EVERYTHING ELSE

None of the following are essential, but in case you need to have an opinion on them:

Clothes Your approach should be that everyday cycling can be done in everyday clothes. All that fancy Lycra, all those ad-branded polyester cycling tops, all those helmets and cleats – it's all just a uniform, donned by those trying to prove something. Commuting, shopping, touring, visiting pubs or friends or your rehabilitation officer – none of these activities requires 'cycling gear'. Not only does this explain why you aren't wearing a luminescent top and Max Wall tights, it can also explain why your trousers are grubby and holed. And why, if you get fed up of sweaty cycling and take the train home instead, you'll have a seat to yourself.

Helmet If worn, may offer some protection in case of an accident, because you had a camera fixed to it.

Kickstand Turns bicycle into handy camera tripod for self-portraits, or long exposures in badly-lit conditions, such as urban cycle tracks.

Plastic bags Make handy saddle-waterproofers. Also, impermeable layers between socks and shoes during downpours. Best not used for putting sandwiches in afterwards. Except petrol-station sandwiches, which may be slightly improved.

Toothbrush Old ones can be recycled as cog-scrubbers.

T-shirts Old ones can be recycled as fortnightly chain-wipes, ending up patterned with black tiger-stripe oil stains. Old T-shirt chain-wipes can be recycled as black tiger-stripe T-shirts.

High-visibility jacket Hard evidence suggesting bright clothing always helps you avoid an accident is, surprisingly, as hard to find as a cyclist in black on a moonless country lane. Nevertheless, most believe that high-visibility clothing helps in dark conditions – to give taxi drivers something to aim at. Some research on motorcyclists suggests it's contrast that best enhances visibility – dark clothing on a bright day, for instance – so maybe cyclists' bulge-revealing Lycra has an unexpected safety role. If you're in a railway station and wearing a high-visibility jacket but not a helmet, people will assume you're staff, and frostily demand to know why the 8.15 to Cambridge is running late. Tell them: 'That's the Cambridge train there; it says next stop Leeds but that's a mistake. Quick, it's about to leave.' Similarly, if you're in a supermarket car park, you can direct the traffic, and they'll go anywhere you point them – even towards a brick wall.

GPS Either you're totally against it (screen too small to show enough of a map, ancient art of map-reading will be lost, etc.) or totally for it (can examine precise movements after a journey and see if better route-finding solution was possible).

Cleats Twist-lock device that joins your feet to the pedals. Either you're totally for them (make uphills magically easier because you can pull pedal up as well as push down, 'that's what every serious cyclist uses', etc.) or, more adventurously, totally against them (shoes with cleats clack on concrete or lino-like high heels – perhaps not the effect you want if you're already wearing tights; also, make up sobering stories of someone who tumbled on their bike before they could twist out, and broke their hip).

Panniers Only admit to having Ortliebs, the German maker and Rolls-Royce of load-carrying. ('I don't know how long they stay totally waterproof and as new – I've only had mine 15 years.') This suggests you're not only a connoisseur of quality, but also a long-term cyclist. However, trad-Britgear fans might try putting the case for Carradice, possibly even saddlebag-only ('my grandad had his till the day he died, aged 102 – kept his Woodbines and brown ale in there, he did').

Computer Even cheap computers now have a bewildering range of functions way beyond the simple disappointment of finding you've only done 12 miles today. They monitor your heart rate, calorie consumption, alcohol intake, bedtime, etc., and generally nag at you to ride faster. Such functions are best switched off. Maintain that your computer cost £4 from Lidl's annual May sale but still has all the functions of someone else's £100 model.

MAINTENANCE, REPAIR, AND HOW TO AVOID BOTH

Cycle maintenance is easy, and can be done yourself with little expense or fuss. Simply put the bike in the back of the car and drive to the nearest bike shop.

There's only one thing you really should do, and that's to wipe your chain with a soft cloth (an old T-shirt is ideal, particularly if it was an unwanted present) and dedicated cleaner (not washing-up liquid – it contains salt) every couple of weeks. It's easy, quick and doubles the life of your chain and gears, so of course nobody ever does it. So either claim to do it or admit you don't, depending on which is likely to impress more.

Here's what to say about mechanical problems:

Punctures 'Straightforward, of course.' Disparage any talk of self-repairing tyres, CO_2 capsules or miracle liquids: the simple craft of manual puncture repair is best. Talk casually about turning the bike upside down, slipping off the back wheel (punctures tend to be on back wheels) and working the tyre off and back on with your hands – tyre levers are for amateurs. It only works for good-quality tyres though, which is why you can't do the trick with other people's. You always carry a spare inner tube – proof of your competence; the holed one goes back home with you where you can patch it at leisure. (Of course, in reality, you never need to demonstrate any of this, thanks to using Kevlar-lined puncture-proof tyres. The mark of a knowledgeable cyclist is that they haven't mended a puncture in 10 years; thanks to the technology, they haven't needed to.)

Brakes 'Trickier than it looks', implying you have developed your craft at adjusting them over the years. Blame any problems – lopsided contact, squeaks, worn blocks, etc. – on 'poor-quality Chinese parts'. If asked to fix someone else's, claim only to be able to fix the other type ('sorry, I only know about V-brakes/disc brakes').

Gears, etc. 'Much trickier than it looks.' Even experienced cyclists will nod in agreement. Best left to the professional mechanic. Cue gripping stories about how you tried in vain to fix your skipping derailleur on a Saturday evening in rural Scotland, and ended up stuck in one inappropriate gear and an appropriate pub until the bike shop opened on Monday morning. Even experienced cyclists will nod in envy.

Wheel truing 'Obviously, one for the experts.' Tweaking the spokes to make a wonky wheel straight (with a spoke key, which looks as though it could bleed radiators) takes years of practice – it's a mystic art only proper bike mechanics know. There's little point in pretending you can true wheels, as nobody will believe you anyway. In fact, the right approach is probably to have a spoke key, but never to have dared use it, like a home plumbing kit.

Comedic bodges Stories of improvised repairs with hopelessly makeshift tools or equipment, miles from anywhere, in a storm, to get you as far as the next bike shop, always go down well. Especially if they didn't really work. Towing a fellow cyclist; hovering precariously over the bare seatpost left by a snapped-off saddle; surviving on one jammed gear or one pedal; or – an old favourite – stuffing a catastrophically ripped tyre with grass, for example.

You can justify anything with comparisons to cycling-friendly Netherlands, a mythical land of car-free bike lanes where the entire population cycles all the time.

HOT TOPICS

To be accepted as a cycling expert, you don't have to talk technical about bikes. (Just as well, if you encounter a recently converted MAMIL in a bar.)

You just need to know a few right answers that will get all the cyclists in your group nodding in agreement and thinking they really ought to buy you a drink as you're clearly the right sort. Carry them off with confidence and the wannabe cyclists will be impressed too.

You won't get far with the anti-cyclists, but they'll probably still be stuck in traffic somewhere, texting.

CYCLING FACILITIES

Always substandard: cycle paths are too narrow, too short, full of glass, and dump you on the main road too soon anyway. There's not enough cycle parking; if there is, it's too cramped, too close to the wall, too far from the entrance. One-way streets should be two-way for cyclists ('as is common on the continent'). On-road cycle lanes are ignored by motorists, taxis, buses, or used as an excuse to pass too closely.

You can claim that any facility 'actually makes it more dangerous for cyclists', while giving other road users, especially the non-cycling councillors who voted it through, the impression that money is being spent on cycling provision. Councils always claim it was installed 'in consultation with the local cycling group'. Which it was – except they ignored the group's feedback that it was a dangerous waste of money.

You can justify anything with comparisons to cycling-friendly Netherlands, a mythical land of car-free bike lanes where the entire population cycles all the time. Refer to some miracle facility you saw online in Groningen or Assen ('40% of all journeys there are by bike compared to 2% here – well, no wonder', etc.).

CYCLING ILLEGALLY ON PAVEMENTS

You don't do it yourself, of course, but, when nobody at all is about, it's clearly justifiable as a way to avoid a dangerous road. Equally clearly, if there's any chance of inconveniencing pedestrians, you should get off and push. Letter writers to local newspapers who complain that cyclists 'all cycle on the pavement', and that a friend of their mother's neighbour was NEARLY KILLED by one, might be advised that it's statistically safer to walk on the road than the pavement. It isn't, but they won't know that.

Pedantry can help, but you might be better off with the damned-if-you-do-damned-if-you-don't line: 'Motorists shout that we shouldn't be on the road, pedestrians shout that we shouldn't be on the pavement.'

MOTORIST V PEDESTRIAN V CYCLIST

These are emphatically not exclusive rival groups; most cyclists are motorists, and we're all pedestrians at some point in the journey. Inciting tribalism is silly and futile. We are all road users; the war is between good and bad users, not modes of transport. We should be working together to make a pleasant and safe public space for all to share.

Having made that Abe Lincoln-like point with a suitable air of gravitas, you can spend the next hour swapping stories about taxis that shouted unprovoked abuse at you, buses that cut you up, motorists that ignore cycle boxes at lights, lorries that overtake you and then turn left, etc. And the pedestrian who stepped out in the road in front of you listening to their iPod. Typical. Motorists, pedestrians, they're all the same.

RED-LIGHT JUMPING (RLJ)

Reckless RLJ is never condoned, of course, and you never do it yourself; but as traffic signals are generally phased with no regard for bikes – at large junctions, or roadworks for instance – there are certainly occasions where judicious RLJ may be necessary. Hint darkly about left-turning HGVs that have turned up to a tight, railed junction after the cyclist got there – it may well be that the only safe thing for a cyclist to do is to flee on red.

Do this sombrely enough, perhaps with implied reference to a recent fatal incident where the cyclist presumably stuck to the law, and you can escape the fact that most RLJers are just impatient.

ROAD TAX

The common complaint, generally shouted or mistyped, that cyclists 'don't pay road tax so shouldn't be on the road' is just about as wrong as any statement can be. Rebuttal is easy but usually ineffective: for the shouters or mistypers, it's whoever repeats themselves long enough wins.

> ## Scoff at any use of the term 'road tax' by anyone in the media, and hold them up to ridicule.

Still, here are some facts to establish your credentials as an informed cyclist:

- Road tax, that is a tax on motorists to pay for roads, was abolished in 1937, on Churchill's initiative.

- Roads are paid for out of general taxation, like schools and hospitals; right of use is not dependent on what you pay, or cigarette smokers could claim more right to hospital use than non-smokers.

- Cyclists have 'right of way' on roads; car drivers can only use them under licence.

- Vehicles pay vehicle excise duty (VED) based on emissions; if bikes were subject to VED they would pay zero, like electric and other low-emission cars (*see* 'Lies, Damned Lies, and…', page 101).

- Most cyclists have a car, so they're not only 'paying road tax' (VED) anyway but are kindly using the bike instead, freeing up space for vehicles.

- Cycles are banned on motorways and a small number of trunk roads – so cyclists don't get to use all the big-budget projects like bypasses which they've paid for out of their taxes.

Scoff at any use of the term 'road tax' by anyone in the media, and hold them up to ridicule. The related argument – that cyclists should be registered with a licence plate, like cars, which would stop all red-light jumping and pavement cycling – is easily demolished too ('Switzerland tried it, didn't work, waste of money, abolished it.'), especially as it's not unknown for car drivers to speed, park illegally, drive uninsured, have accidents, etc.

NAKED STREETS

No, this doesn't refer to riding unclothed (that's the worldwide annual World Naked Bike Ride). A 'naked street' has no road markings, signs or signals, and is a free-for-all area where motor traffic, pedestrians and cyclists – having to work out all their encounters individually – all therefore mix slowly and safely. You can claim it is 'common in the Netherlands' where it 'works fine'.

THE BLUFFER'S GUIDE TO CYCLING

Or the opposite; hardly anybody you meet will have seen a real one. Certainly not in England, whose much-hyped example – Exhibition Road in Kensington, London – is about as naked as Scott of the Antarctic, and functions as a normal busy street with distinct car space, pavements and no bike parking. Use this to prove your argument either way.

INSURANCE

This one comes up in papers occasionally, usually as a scare story telling motorists that 'Europe' is considering 'making any collision between car and cycle the motorist's fault'. Nonsense, you say; on the continent there's merely a presumed insurance protection towards the more vulnerable road user. In, say, a pedestrian-cyclist clash, the cyclist's insurance will pay for damages unless they can show the cyclist was not at fault. The same tends to be true for car-bike collisions. ('It works perfectly well all over the continent, and makes for much more mutual respect on the roads…and pavements'.)

SMUG CYCLISTS

The standard reproof from motorists masking their guilt about taking half an hour to drive a mile to work: cyclists are smug. Not true: we cyclists are simply pleased with ourselves, because we're clearly superior to everyone else.

MORE CONTENTIOUS TOPICS

The aforementioned topics have a strong consensus among cyclists, and you can safely take the standard view given. However, there are a few matters where even cyclists disagree. Here are the main ones.

SEPARATED V INTEGRATED FACILITIES

Should we be agitating for a Netherlands-style system of wide, separated, traffic-free bike lanes, with their own junctions and lights, priority over motor vehicles, etc., even if a lane of traffic must be converted to do so? Or do we concentrate on improving existing roads such that cyclists mix with traffic in a much safer and more attractive way? Clearly the first is better but equally clearly will never happen, so that viewpoint suits the idealist, bolshy type who writes long anonymous campaigning blogs. The second is much more practical but will equally never happen, so suits the idealist, bolshy type who writes long anonymous campaigning blogs.

CRITICAL MASS

Large 'spontaneous' gatherings of cyclists in a major city centre (London's is monthly, on the South Bank) who cycle around slowly for an hour or so, stopping traffic briefly as they do. Benign show of strength in numbers that delays people for only a few seconds? Or irritating gathering of hippy troublemakers with horrible music booming from their cycle-trailer sound systems? No point asking the question during the ride – you won't be able to hear anything thanks to the horrible music booming from their cycle-trailer sound systems.

HELMETS

A contentious topic – so touchy that for many cyclists it's a subject to avoid, like politics or religion, at convivial dinner parties. The best way to avoid damage to your head is to avoid talking about them. Steer the conversation away accordingly: 'Well, I'm sure we all have our own views…By the way, have you seen that ridiculous new bike lane at the end of town?', etc.

However, if you are up for a fight – and there are plenty of people who are so concerned for your safety that, if you say on an internet forum you have no intention of wearing a helmet, they'll threaten you with physical violence – here are a few guidelines for the dreaded helmet conversation.

First, choose where you stand on helmets – not too abruptly or they'll crack though; they're flimsier than most think – then look at only the evidence which supports your view. (Which is what most people do most of the time anyway.) It surprises some cycling beginners that most experienced cyclists are anti-compulsion, and often very wary about helmets.

Pro-helmet compulsion
With most people, certainly nervous or beginner cyclists, you don't have to make a case. They're scared enough as

it is. Helmet wearing is common sense, like seat belts, so should be compulsory. Once you came off and your helmet split in two but your head was unscathed. And you once went out with a nurse, so that settles it. That'll be plenty to convince most people.

Pro-helmet but anti-compulsion
Yes, helmets do offer protection in certain circumstances, but so do bulletproof jackets – that's no reason to make them compulsory. It's a balance of personal freedom and choice and not creating a climate of fear. There's safety in numbers – the countries with the lowest rates of helmet-wearing, such as the Netherlands, are also the safest for cycling. Overall, helmet compulsion increases mortality because fewer people cycle, therefore more die early through heart attacks, etc. In Australia, when they made them mandatory, the rate of head injuries went up, which proves it. That makes you sound knowledgeable but reasonable. (*See* 'Lies, Damned Lies, and…', page 101.)

Not pro-helmet
Helmets offer only marginal protection at best – essentially, for a child falling off a stationary bike onto a road. They distract from the real issues of good facilities and safe cycling, which have an overwhelmingly greater effect on safety. They're not a magic shield of invincibility, as many cyclists seem to think as they hurtle through red lights or sneak up the side of an HGV. The 'split helmet saved my life' story is a fallacy: the split helmet failed, transferring all the shock to the head, so what saved you was your skull. Always, therefore, cycle

with a skull. And in fact, helmets can cause accidents: research shows that helmet-wearers are passed more closely and dangerously by vehicles than non-wearers. Cycling bodies such as the CTC are neutral on helmet-wearing and solidly anti-compulsion, which proves it. This is the most correct view, but the least believed, so approach with care.

Whichever viewpoint you hold, it's good to blind people with science. Look up a study at random online and quote any figure out of context. ('According to Thompson, Rivara and Thompson in 1996...', or 'Walker, in 2007, found that...' for example, followed by any clinching stat from 'Lies, Damned Lies, and...', page 101. Or mention the difference between 1980s Snell standard helmets and the less-stringent British Standard helmets which replaced them, and use this to prove your argument either way.

EVERYDAY RIDING

Going by bike, council leaflets endlessly remind us, is cheap, green, healthy and fun. You know better. Depending on the sort of riding people have in mind, it's often none of these things. Here's why, for each sort of cycling, in descending order of popularity:

Leisure Based on driving bikes to nearest family friendly, traffic-free trail two hours away. By definition, unnecessary, hence environmentally irresponsible, and leisurely, hence of limited health benefit, especially when cream tea is factored in.

Mountain biking Same as 'Leisure', but with more processing of altitude and mud; hence more environmental cost in showers, washing, taxis to outpatients, etc.

Training and sport The most popularly enforced image. Centred around fantasy kit reviewed in glossy magazines and punishing exercise regimes. Expensive and painful.

Charity rides Worst of all worlds: air-fuel-gobbling ways of portraying cycle touring as a rigorously paid penance that friends are guilted into subsidising. But at least it benefits poor people in a deprived area – two office staff and an intern in the charity's grim West Midlands office. Expensive, unecological, stressful, unpleasant. Very popular.

Touring The second-best sort of cycling, with only minor question marks over (say) unecological long-haul flights or the expense of rain-necessitated hotels. But the most authentic way to travel the world with freedom, exploring primitive, remote back lanes far from civilisation, such as the Sustrans route (*see* page 72) to the town centre.

Whereas…everyday riding has a dull media image and no advertising revenue, so it's largely ignored. But it's the only genuinely good sort of cycling: commuting and general A-to-B riding around town on simple, cheap machines that saves motorised journeys and makes urban spaces much more agreeable. Dismiss other types of riding as irrelevant hobbyism.

WHERE TO RIDE

People will want to believe that you go everywhere by bike: you're a genuine utility cyclist, an everyday rider. The approach is always casual and matter of fact: of course you cycle to work, or to the shops, or to hear your sentence pronounced – by bike is the fastest, most convenient way, with no traffic jams or parking worries.

Smile and shrug as if to say, only an idiot would go by car. Don't be too intense, or the dry, comfortable car driver with knife-creased trousers may seem more appealing.

Demonstrate familiarity with A-to-B cycling around Britain and, ideally, abroad – and know the best and worst places to do so.

RURAL BRITAIN

This is easily summarised by road types:

Motorways The safest places of all for cycling, with zero cycling casualties, largely because you're not allowed to. There are, however, places where cycle lanes run alongside motorways – the M48 Severn Bridge, for example, where you can even cycle into the services – to give you that autobahn feel.

A-roads Most direct but most dangerous roads, despite the tempting wide shoulders to cycle in, thanks to the HGVs tornadoing past you. The chances of a cycling accident on A-roads are four times higher than on other roads, so they're best avoided; except that a B-road detour will take four times as long. The most lethal sections are (a) the junctions and (b) the stretches in-between.

B-roads Surprisingly dangerous, thanks to copious bends round phantom obstacles and roller-coaster topography, plus speeding locals who 'know the road', so there can't possibly be a cyclist round that corner or over that brow.

Country lanes Generally pleasant ribbons of tarmac that wind o'er dale and lea through cake-stop villages. Sparsely trafficked save for tractors, and the local cycling club whizzing through in a peloton to beat you to the cake stop and occupy entire café. Surface pretty good except at cattle crossings, where you cycle through a load of old cow muck. Almost any thin yellow line on an OS map, especially with a dotted border, can be confidently described as 'lovely, quiet, little-known back route through charming villages'.

URBAN BRITAIN

This is also easily summarised, and similar to the country lanes experience above. Not the bit about being pleasant, though – the bit about the cattle crossings, metaphorically.

British towns and cities are generally terrible for cycling. The few places with a recognisably friendly cycling culture (in the sense of a bad-tempered, grudge 'friendly' football match) include Cambridge and York, while London has a strong cycling contingent out of sheer bloody-mindedness.

Otherwise you can dismiss pretty much anywhere else as having a couple of nice leisure river or canalside routes which don't go anywhere useful, but the city centre itself is car-oriented and hostile to two wheels, with a worse-than-useless patchwork of substandard cycle tracks and lanes put in by a clueless council. You'll never be far wrong.

It's all about money, you can say: we spend under £1.50 a head per year on cycle infrastructure outside

London, where major cities have in total under 20 miles of segregated urban cycleways.

Here's what to say about selected towns and cities:

London
In the capital's centre, this is the most visible cycling contingent in the UK, because (unlike Cambridge) most people wear reflective jackets the colour of lemon toilet cleaner. Even in the daytime.

Helmets are very common in London, usually so people can fix cameras to them to use in evidence later.

There's a strong commuter focus, typically a young male or female with work clothes in a rucksack. The most popular bike is a top-end road model, but you don't get time to see which brand as he or she flashes past through the red light in front of you. There are many 'folders' in the City of London ridden by smart types in suits, which tells you something – they earn enough to afford a Brompton.

Helmets are very common, usually so people can fix cameras to them to use in evidence later. There's a high-pressure, competitive road culture: all traffic is in a hurry and there's a constant conflict for road space between taxis, buses, cars, cyclists, pedestrians, ambulances. Indeed, as previously mentioned, some more aggressive couriers carry a heavy lock on the handlebars to use as a weapon should a driver incur their displeasure. Hitting a vehicle, no matter under what provocation, is not something the bluffer should ever condone. It could damage the lock.

London has two showpiece cycling infrastructures unique in the UK:

1. **Boris bikes (Santander Cycle Hire)**. See city bikes, pages 41/42

2. **Cycle Superhighways** (CS) Network of cycle paths supposedly providing safe, fast routes through the capital, though most consist solely of blue paint and are more colloquially referred to as 'car parking'. Two stretches, however, form Britain's best urban cycle routes, and the nearest we have to Dutch-style segregated facilities: the bit of CS6 from Elephant & Castle to Blackfriars and soon to King's Cross ('the North-South CS'); and the bit of CS3 paralleling the Thames between Westminster and Tower Bridge ('the East-West CS') – one of the world's great urban rides offering all the postcard sights, so it's easy to imply you've ridden it even if you haven't. The London Cycling Campaign lobbies for better facilities. Either diss it ('middle-aged, tired, lost its radical 1980s mojo') or praise it ('professional, effective, grown-up at last.'). The people who actually pressurise councils to change things for cyclists, you can maintain, are the borough campaigning

groups such as Southwark, Islington or Hackney. That makes you sound worthily involved with campaigning and activism, not just someone who simply sits on their backside. (Though, in fact, sitting down is precisely what 'activists' do, [a] in dull council meetings [b] writing letters and emails to MPs and councils and [c] attending consultation sessions on new developments.)

Cambridge

Britain's best cycling city, with a strong culture of utility cycling. Little Lycra and few helmets, but lots of normal clothes, and a healthy proportion of tweed and baskets carrying Dostoyevsky or PhD gene research. Obviously, in term time, many of those are students hurrying to avoid a lecture. The streets and lanes are packed with bikes – it's the nearest a British cyclist gets to the Netherlands. (Except perhaps Hull, but that's only because you can get a ferry.)

Decent cycling infrastructure, by UK standards, including an odd 14-mile piste alongside a guided busway to St Ives. Also, partly thanks to tech-savvy graduates, the country's most accomplished local cycle campaign. (Drop random first names to suggest familiarity and reflected glory: 'I bumped into Martin and Simon from the Cycling Campaign the other day…')

Pooh-pooh anyone who tries to explain it all by flatness; students; eco-educated, young, nano-tech commuters; or small-town scale. These are all factors, but you will maintain that Cambridge simply has a self-sustaining cycle culture: people cycle because people cycle, a critical-mass effect that any other town could replicate if the political will were there. Which it never is, so you'll never be proved wrong.

York

A notch or two down from Cambridge, but a similar bikey-historic-town feel. However, you can't cycle in the pedestrianised historic centre during daytime, which is probably when you want to. Not that you could anyway, thanks to the pedestrian zone being clogged with cars sporting disabled badges. York is a great ecclesiastical centre of course, and miracles still occur: the lame get out of such cars and can suddenly walk to M&S unaided.

Selected other places

Bristol Boasts one of Britain's highest spends on cycle infrastructure per head: £25, over half a typical Dutch figure. Shame the facilities aren't half as good..

Newcastle Improving slowly. Fine riverside cycleway under those majestic bridges, cyclist tunnel under the Tyne, and new 'superhighway' in John Dobson Street. And lots of Greggs.

Liverpool Fine promenade paths either side of the Mersey Ferry and some useful urban routes, because they provide quick escape.

Leeds New Cycle Superhighway links centre to Bradford, but pale imitation of London's best. Uncleared snowy stretches in winter mean bonus sledging possibilities.

Birmingham Comprehensive canal path network, but rough surfaces mean narrowboat may be quicker. City network up to normal UK standards; i.e., terrible.

Manchester Mysteriously rated by a 2010 Campaign for Better Transport report as better for bikes than Cambridge; perhaps misprinted 'bikes' as 'Nikes'.

Edinburgh Tramlines can be a menace, but at least the threat of being run over by a tram is slim, thanks to the unlikelihood of the system ever being finished. An active local cycle campaign, nice circuit round Arthur's Seat, a few decent tracks.

Milton Keynes Despite the much-vaunted system of separate cycle tracks, it is one of the most car-dependent big towns in the UK. (Speculate on role of concrete cows in this.) Same applies to Stevenage.

Nottingham Least car-dependent big town in the UK. Speculate on the role of the gender imbalance myth (urban legend that more single women live here than anywhere else) in all this.

Warrington Renowned cycle campaign whose website features amusingly bad cycle facilities every month.

ABROAD

You're not just well acquainted with the cool capitals – you know about cycling in them too, which is even cooler.

Most people want to sound well travelled, so entire conversations can take place about, say, Barcelona's beachside cycle track, with nobody admitting they've never actually been there.

Amsterdam

Good (but not perfect) network of tracks and paths, but most important, a relaxed, fear-free and enjoyable place to cycle where bikes are mainstream transport. Speculate on the role of 'coffee shops' in all this. (Or, more plausibly, pro-cycling policies that followed safety campaigns in the 1970s and 1980s.) However, even cooler is to cite obscure Dutch towns with unimaginably high rates of cycling, the more unpronounceable the better: Groningen, 's-Hertogenbosch, Tytsjerksteradiel, etc.

Copenhagen

Well-established bike culture and infrastructure. As with Amsterdam, normal clothes rule; helmets and Lycra unknown. Child-trailers and 'Christiania bikes' (cargo bikes with huge front boxes) common. Speculate on role of Christiania (soft-drugs hippy district) in all this. Gradually declining rates of cycling, however; speculate on role of pastries, exorbitantly priced beer, etc. in all that.

Paris

As patchy and confusing as London in terms of infrastructure, but the well-established Vélib' bike hire scheme is popular, perhaps because if you do cycle through some dog turds, you just switch to another bike.

Barcelona

From nothing, this has become an ultra-cool cycling destination in a handful of years. The old town has many naked streets and semi-naked cyclists, on 'Bicing' bikes, the locals' hire scheme. Skeletal but useful system of separated cycle tracks, and lovely beachside/promenade path. Illegal pavement cycling abounds with apparently no consequence; speculate on role of €2 bottles of wine in all this.

Berlin

Not quite as cool as Barcelona, but cooler than Paris. Wide range of ages, genders, hairstyles, piercings, etc. in a strong, green-conscious cycling culture. Speculate on the role of trendy little bars in artily restored old Communist blocks in all this. However, even cooler is to cite more obscure towns with even greener reputations: Münster, Freiburg, etc.

Trondheim

Famous for its unique bike lift, a tiny escalator that you put one foot on while wheeling your bike up a notoriously steep hill. Speculate on places in Britain at the top of a steep hill that could do with one, such as any youth hostel.

USA

The spiritual home of the gas guzzler has some surprisingly green oases of cycle use. Eco-conscious Portland, Oregon is pretty well known ('Some great traffic-free boulevards down the east side – no wonder cycle commuting's gone up sixfold – Britain could learn', etc.). San Francisco and New York have some of the most important markers of a strong cycling culture in America – outspoken bloggers, crazy couriers, and YouTube videos showing police prejudice against cyclists. But one claimant to the title of best US biking city is a surprise to many, hence good bluffing fodder: cold, snowy, northern Minneapolis, where the January average is -10°C. Speculate on the role of Minnesota's hardy Scandinavian heritage in all this.

Tokyo
Lots of utility cycling, most of it illegally on pavements by people on shopping bikes, weaving between suited office workers. Speculate on the role of mother-and-child bikes that cost as little as a bottle of house red in all this (though note that a bottle of house red can cost as much as a bike).

Taipei
Taiwan's capital had a problem with pavement cycling, so they simply legalised it, solving the problem at a stroke. Has excellent, long riverside cycle tracks, including toilets specially made to take bicycles inside with you. Cycle-friendly country, and probably made your bike's frame. Speculate on role of Asian social discipline in all this.

Bogotá
Every Sunday and public holiday, long sections of the Colombian capital's roads are closed off to traffic for the

'Ciclovía'. Cyclists, walkers, skaters, wheelchair users and so on can ride many miles traffic-free. Pop-up stalls serve food, drinks, dance lessons, etc. Lament fact that our equivalents are feeble in comparison and have to be corporately supported. Speculate on role of South American social spontaneity in all this.

Your choice
Pick any city you know. Whether well-used or empty, chaotic or ordered, its cycle facilities and cycling culture can support any point you want. ('Manila's got no cycle lanes, and it's the world's most congested city, which proves...'; 'Dubai's got some superb cycle lanes but nobody uses them, which shows...'; 'Seattle's city bike hire scheme closed because of their mandatory helmet laws, which demonstrates...'; etc.) Drop in any arcane local knowledge you have, or can make up, and speculate on its significance.

CYCLE-CAFES
The rise in cycle-cafes is a gift for the bluffer, as it makes you sound knowledgeable about cycling when it's really the cafe you're talking about.

There are two types of independent cycle-cafe. The traditional one is the village, mug-of-tea, home-made sponge-cake sort of place, often a regular haunt of club cyclists and located off the beaten track. Name-drop a few of these (Eureka! in the Wirral, a club hub since 1928, or the Dalesman in Gargrave, North Yorks, for instance) and people will think you're a hugely travelled cyclist. *Typically overheard remark:* 'I've been coming here since before June behind the counter there was married. She's a grandmother now...'.

The more modern one is the urban-chic bike-shop-with-integral-cyber-cafe. You can get your wheel trued en route to work, enjoy a barista espresso, and update your Facebook status. The walls will be decorated with fixies (see 'Glossary', page 128) and there'll be a selection of niche, artsy cycling magazines for browsing. The archetype is Look Mum No Hands! in central London's Old Street, opened in 2010, though knowledge of Bristol's much older Mud Dock Cafe ('of course, they were ahead of the game 20 years ago...') will impress. *Typically overheard remark:* 'So I told the CEO, if you don't let me bring my Pinarello into the office, I'll go and work for Apple instead...'.

There's no shame in mentioning chains, though: many a club run is targeted around a Costa or Starbucks, and most cyclists – being bargain-conscious – will admire the good deal you claim to have got at say Greggs ('Bacon sarnie and coffee for two quid! Just the thing to start a day's ride!') or Wetherspoon's ('Three quid for a cooked breakfast, including a free pint! Just the thing to start a day's ride!').

Actually, you don't even need to go into any cafes to know how good they are. Just look for the road bikes stacked up outside on a Sunday afternoon. The more bikes, the better the cake.

ON ROAD AND TRACK

Cycling is the best way to see the world, from many different perspectives – thrilling mountain passes, unspoilt local villages, bus shelters waiting for the rain to stop – and the more of Britain and the world people think you've explored in the saddle, the more they'll admire your apparent wisdom and experience.

The only question non-cyclists can think of to ask is how many miles a day you do. 'Oh, only about 40', is the right sort of answer – far enough to impress, but at only four hours or so of actual cycling, it leaves plenty of time for 'sightseeing'. (In practice, the insides of WiFi-cafes, bars, cheap hotels and bike shops.)

NATIONAL CYCLE NETWORK (NCN)

This isn't quite as impressive as it sounds. Rather than a grand Dutch-style system of car-free paths that can take you anywhere, it's a system of signposts that link a hotchpotch of roads (which form 70% of the NCN), rail trails, canal towpaths, bridleways, cycle paths and over-engineered junctions with CYCLISTS DISMOUNT signs.

The network is numbered similarly to roads, so that NCN1 goes from Dover to Shetland, and NCN4 goes from London to St Davids on the toe of the Welsh coast. The surface is variable though: one section of NCN4 is the scenic, flat, tarmac, car-free, useful Bristol and Bath Railway Path (*see* page 76) while NCN1 between Whitby and Scarborough is out of this world – as in, rocky lunar surface.

The NCN system was the creation of Sustrans, a charity promoting sustainable transport. Follow the fashion by starting off praising its achievements, then list specific problems with the routes you know at length.

Particularly popular complaints are the mystery diversions, where the route takes you round three sides of a square for no apparent reason; closure conundrums, where a vital part of the path is shut off by works, with no signed alternative; overgrown paths; abrupt transitions from quiet car-free path to fast main road; wildly inconsistent surface quality; missing signs; motorbike-blocking gates that unfortunately block all but the narrowest cyclists too; and so on. Pick two or three, be vague about their location, and say they ruin your local path, which would otherwise be a wonderful resource. You'll never be far wrong.

CANAL TOWPATHS

Less promising than they sound. Yes, they're mostly flat (though there's the odd hefty hill-climb, such as Five Rise Locks at Bingley, and the occasional long slope, such as Caen Hill outside Devizes, with its staircase of 16 or so locks). Yes, they're mostly traffic-free. And yes, they link enticing end points, such as Leeds–Liverpool, or London–Birmingham (on the Grand Union). And in London, Regent's Canal and its offshoots provide neat, decently surfaced, traffic-free corridors across the capital.

In practice, though, most towpaths are stony and puddled, and the scenery is often drab. You can see a lot of native wild animals, though in run-down city margins, they're the sort that throw stones at you. There are also many stretches where the Canal & River Trust doesn't allow you to cycle, such as on the astonishingly precarious aqueduct at Pontcysyllte, near Llangollen. That doesn't stop locals from riding insouciantly along the flying ledge while texting their friends.

RAIL TRAILS

The rural cobweb of Beeching-axed lines looks like it only needs a bit of tarmac to make it an ideal cycle path network – flat, car-free, sometimes in lovely scenery. Problems are many though: uselessly remote locations, decayed bridges or viaducts, road crossings, and housing estates or factories blocking your way. In practice, there are a few gems (below), but also a lot of muddy, overgrown trails to nowhere, not worth rehabilitating.

BEST ROUTES

There are a few routes that, as a proper cyclist, everyone will think you have done. Don't disappoint them. Make sure they do think you have done them.

Camel Trail

Rail trail way out west: 10 miles of beautiful, estuaryside, car-free rail trail to Padstow harbour. Family favourite for peace and solitude, and hence jammed solid with wobbling hire bikes and yelling kids in summer. Shun the expensive cliché of a Rick Stein restaurant at the end, explaining that you found a little-known bistro serving wonderful, cheap fish 'straight off the boat'.

There are a few routes that, as a proper cyclist, everyone will think you have done. Don't disappoint them. Make sure they do think you have done them.

Bristol and Bath Railway Path

Sustrans's first and most successful big project, dating from the mid-1980s. Lovely river scenery, car-free and a useful 13-mile-long link between the two cities. Spoilt by the ring road slicing it in two. This is the UK's best cycle path. Tell that to the Dutch; they'll sympathise.

Thames Path

Doesn't remotely compare to the great German riverside paths. Apart from a few glorious off-road stretches (between Hammersmith and Staines, and between Tower Bridge and Erith), it is mainly on-road with traffic, nowhere near the river. The success of *Three Men in a Boat* shows British priorities: we don't use rivers for cycle paths, we use them for writing comic travelogues.

Coast to Coast (C2C)

Three-day, 135-mile, variety-pack pearl of a trip from Whitehaven (or Workington) on the Cumbrian coast to Sunderland (or Newcastle) and the North Sea. Expect medium-strength challenges en route (Pennine hills, finding accommodation, bribing a friend to be support driver) and a great sense of achievement; but it's within reach of anyone fit enough to, say, lug their bike across the Carlisle station footbridge. This is a charity fundraising staple that raises millions for good causes, such as repairing the environmental damage to cotton-producing countries ravaged by demand for promotional T-shirts used on trip.

Land's End to John o'Groats (LEJOG)

The traditional 'ultimate challenge' (usually this direction, to tap into prevailing winds) has no single standard route, and so can be any distance from 875 miles or so up. The record time is 44 hours; fast club riders often do it as a group in a week with a van carrying their luggage; solo riders carrying their gear might take two weeks, plus another waiting for a vacant bike space on the homeward train from Thurso.

Notorious problems include the sawtooth Devon hills, blatantly lying distance signs, the long slog up the A6 to Shap, the lorry that nearly ran you off the road outside Manchester, the rainiest week for 136 years, the novelty of cooked breakfast every morning soon wearing off. But

THE BLUFFER'S GUIDE TO CYCLING

talk about the amazing experience, getting the measure of your island, progression of scenery, wonderful people you meet, etc. All exaggerated of course; you only meet people while they're serving you a toasted sandwich or fixing your derailleur, and the best scenery is on the B&B placemats. Nevertheless, this is an achievement that commands respect, so milk it: almost any future anecdote can begin 'one time, while I was doing my end to end…'

Dunwich Dynamo

An annual event rather than a route, but a must-be-believed-to-have-done through-the-night mass ride on midsummer Saturday, starting at a Hackney pub around 8pm and ending at Dunwich beach 120 miles away the next morning. Not organised, not for charity, not sponsored, and hence a much-loved cult London ride that has now gone mainstream, with thousands of participants. Talk about the 'amazing high' from cycling en masse through silent, dark country lanes, following long lines of blinking rear lights, 2am 'lunch' stop at specially opened village halls, and the genuinely simple, joyous, celebration-of-cycling feel of this uncommercialised event.

The main talking point is the extraordinary bikes you saw people doing it on (dog in basket, shopping bike, unicycle, tandem recumbent tricycle, etc.), being sure to add that they 'were overtaking' Lycra-clad ironmen on their fancy racing bikes.

OTHER COAST-TO-COAST ROUTES

Trans Pennine Trail

215-mile patchwork of canals, rail trails, towpaths, roads, taking you from Southport to the sparse coastal prairies east of Hull. Easier and flatter than you expect, and rather duller, especially east of Doncaster. That has the advantage of making Hull feel like a vibrant, stylish and cosmopolitan metropolis though.

Way of the Roses

Morecambe to Bridlington: a surprise contender for 'most popular alternative to C2C'. It starts well with a promenade path and statue of Eric Morecambe, then bold scenery; the eastern third is dull, with a two-mile detour to see a coffee machine installed a couple of miles before Driffield (where there's proper coffee), but the David Hockney connection at the end has helped (many of his recent paintings are landscapes of this part of the world). Nice station at Bridlington, with an outstanding feature: frequent services out.

Hadrian's Cycleway

This takes perverse pleasure in avoiding the Wall itself. Fewer hills than expected. A good insight into a harsh, ancient way of life though, especially Carlisle and Newcastle town centres on Saturday night.

Reivers Route

Roughly parallels Hadrian's. An unwieldy combination

of half-interesting roads and bumpy, MTB-only forest tracks near Kielder. Named after pre-1600s sheep and cattle rustlers whose spelling was evidently as arbitrary as the route.

FAMOUS CHALLENGES ABROAD

North Sea Route
The world's longest signed cycle route: 3,700 miles round the North Sea coast, from East Anglian and Dutch lowlands to Norwegian mountains. It used to be circular, but the 2007 closure of the Lerwick-Bergen ferry spoiled that. Only to be tackled if you have done the right preparation – that is, set up your book deal in advance.

Danube Cycle Path
Lovely, well-surfaced, scenic downhill route around 1,700 miles from Donaueschingen to the Black Sea through nine countries (Germany, Austria, Slovakia, Hungary, Croatia, Serbia, Romania, Bulgaria and Ukraine). It is deservedly popular and well set up for cycle tourism (plentiful cheap accommodation, food, bike shops, etc.).

Nullarbor Plain
Two-week-or-so Australian slog avoiding road trains and looking for water along the Eyre Highway. Either a punishing, pointless trial that makes people think you're mad, or an astounding wilderness adventure that makes people think you're mad.

Pan-American Highway

A 30,000-mile road system from Alaska to Tierra del Fuego, split by a 50-mile gap of Panamanian rainforest in the middle. It takes up to a year or more and is for very adventurous cyclists with the time to do it. Also for bluffers with the time to talk about planning to do it (before going to Belgium for a bank holiday weekend instead).

Round the world

A vague but popular plan that most touring cyclists will 'definitely' do one day, just as soon as the kids grow up/that redundancy comes/I've finally saved up enough – in other words – never. The 'plan' consists only of speculative web surfing, so you can easily join in without committing yourself to anything. There's a current boom in trying to beat the record for a global circumnavigation by bike, mainly by British cyclists with all the requisite skills: survival knowledge, bike maintenance, high fitness, and most important of all, camerawork for the subsequent DVD, and a good interview technique for print and broadcast media afterwards.

MOUNTAIN BIKING

MTB-ing is a distinctive enough activity to have a cult of its own, so don't be too ambitious in your bluffing. Like the activity itself, it's best to stick to a simple line, and keep a low profile. Don't worry too much about the jargon; just check a magazine to see what's in fashion this month.

Do use the word 'technical' frequently though, to

mean 'difficult for most people but not for me'. For example, when talking about colour-coded trails:

Green 'The kids loved it. Nothing technical about it at all.'

Blue 'My missus/boyfriend/dad loved it. Hardly anything technical.'

Red 'I loved it. A few technical bits, but nothing the bike couldn't handle.'

Black 'As soon as the cast comes off, I'll be right back on those technical bits.'

There are several well-known areas with mountain biking trails, such as Coed-y-Brenin in north Wales (the most venerable), Dalby Forest in North Yorkshire, and Kielder Forest in Northumberland. Pick one and claim its particular scenery/accessibility/trail quality balance is by far the best.

Otherwise, talk vaguely about the 'little-known' bridleways and off-road trails in your own locality which are 'actually fantastic' for mountain biking with some 'brilliant downhills' and 'amazing drop-offs' and where you go 'most weekends' with 'your mates'. Keep a muddy mountain bike in the garage to suggest you've actually done some of them, preferably with a buckled back wheel to explain why you can't go anywhere on it at the moment, pending repair.

CLUB CYCLING

Clubs form the backbone of active recreational cycling, probably one bent by thousands of hours hunched over the handlebars. There are over a thousand in the UK; an internet search will likely reveal several near you. Don't be put off by a flimsy or even non-existent website: quality of online presence is no guide to quality of club experience. Except of course for Cambridge CTC, whose outstanding website would be the envy of many a top-rank IT professional, if it weren't for the fact that half its members *are* top-rank IT professionals.

The majority of cycling club members are male, middle-aged or retired; some clubs have women-only branches or associates. Beware guessing ages: club cyclists tend to look a decade younger than they are, partly through so much exercise, partly as they spend so much time smiling.

Some clubs are more intense than others, but the vast majority are friendly and welcoming and all will arrange regular rides – at least a couple a week – ranging from high-speed, mountainous, 90-mile, six-hour morning trips sustained solely by a half-hour tea and cake stop, to short leisurely pootles around a flat local rail trail with the opposite riding/cake time ratio. As riders tend to wear the same gear (helmet, shades, reflective jackets, etc.), it's often hard to tell which sort of rider they are, which is excellent news for the bluffer. You can participate in whichever level of exertion you like, but anyone outside the club will assume that you do those 90-mile jaunts as a matter of routine.

Club riders are always happy to share their knowledge – about technical matters such as hydraulic disc brake maintenance, or more vital issues such as the best local cake-and-coffee deal – whether you asked for it or not. Cafes are a good subject to concentrate on, especially within a club setting. While you may be looked at askance if you (say) don't wear a helmet or know what clipless pedals are, nobody will mind a controversial or contrary opinion on a local cafe.

They'll also tell you about the inevitable club personalities: the fussy organiser, the former time-trial champion, the local media celeb, the still-active octogenarian, the joker, the over-enthusiastic recent convert to cycling with all the gear and no idea. Again, very good for the bluffer: simply listen as you ride alongside them and you'll pick up expertise without effort.

Useful phrases: 'Yes, fixing that's not as simple as it looks, is it?'; 'Fabulous home-made apple crumble there, isn't it?'; 'Oh, him, he's quite a character, isn't he?'.

SPORTS CYCLING

Unless you have a clothes-peg physique, taciturn intensity, and a suspiciously deep knowledge of the pharmaceuticals Lance Armstrong clearly took/didn't take, it'll be obvious you're not a racing cyclist.

So it's best to restrict your bluffing to an 'I tried that once – nearly killed me' sort of approach for the dabbler-friendly events.

Audax rides

Long (often over 100 miles), fast, organised road routes to be completed within a set time. Not races, and with no published 'finishing order': just you against the clock. And the wind, passing lorries, sore backside and wrists, and 'told-you-so' warnings of your partner. The name is from the Latin root for 'audacious', and sometimes called by the French term *randonnée*.

Sportives

Semi-competitive events, somewhere between organised road races and Audaxes. Pick one of the more challenging but popular ones from the Internet; for example, the Fred Whitton Challenge, a 112-mile day ride round the steepest bits of the Lake District. Then drop it casually into conversation: 'I was out last night training for the Fred, and…' or 'I need a new bike for when I do the Fred next May…', etc. Because it's challenging, this will impress people, but because it's popular, you'll be 'gutted' to find you didn't get a place on it.

Tour de France

See it the authentic French way – on TV, in a bar, complaining that today's riders are not a patch on the old ones who would stop for a three-course lunch with wine halfway up an Alp. The yellow jersey – the overall winner of the three-week, 2,000-mile marathon – is the one with the quickest total time; though beefy sprinters might win many flat stages, they comparatively struggle up hills, so winners are usually fighters rather than pure speedsters.

Other awards include the King of the Mountains. Tactics – lowly riders providing human windshields to help star teammates, and timing of breaks – are highly complex; too complex to explain, though you understand them, you imply. Even a little knowledge will impress racing-illiterate British sports fans: that not only did British riders win five of the six Tours between 2013 and 2017, but that a French rider hasn't won the race since 1985, or that the Mountain King's polka-dot jersey echoes the chocolate wrappers of the historical sponsor, Chocolat Poulain.

TRACK CYCLING

Track cycling, being small-scale but varied, eccentric and largely indoors, is currently dominated by Britain. It won seven out of 10 possible Olympic golds at both Beijing 2008 and London 2012 – despite a rule change restricting countries to only one entrant per event which looked suspiciously targeted against its strength in depth. Track sprinter Sir Chris Hoy, with seven medals in total, including six golds, shares the title of Britain's highest-winning Olympian ever with Sir Bradley Wiggins.

A quick guide to some types of race:

Match sprint Bipolar event for two riders. Whoever's leading on the last lap is usually overtaken by the one behind, who's been conserving energy in the slipstream. Hence the wobbly slow cycling up to the abrupt final dash, trying to fool the other rider into going first.

Team pursuit Two teams of four start on opposite sides of the track, aiming to catch the other, or finish the set number of laps first.

Omnium Six-event points competition of bewildering complexity; equivalent of athletics' decathlon.

Keirin 'Kay-rin', Japanese for 'racing wheels'; weird hybrid conceived for betting purposes in 1948. After five laps following an accelerating motorbike called a 'derny', it departs, leaving a sprint finish.

Madison Cross between tag wrestling and the marathon. For an hour or more teams race, one rider at a time until they get tired and are replaced by a teammate, with points awarded for winners of intermediate stages. Named after the first Madison Square Garden in New York. Dumped from Olympics ahead of 2012.

'Get a bicycle. You will not regret it, if you live.'

PEDALLING PEOPLE

FROM ELGAR TO EINSTEIN, MERCKX TO MADONNA

Any listing of celebs who have at one point been photographed pedalling something is sad proof of the niche nature of cycling. There are no lists of celebrity car drivers or famous people who walk to the shops, after all. Nevertheless, such things can be useful. Showing that an idol of the 'cyclophobe' actually rides a bike might help point out to them the error of their ways. For example, when the cyclist-baiting white van man who fancies Katy Perry finds out she rides a bike, he might change his mind, and stop fancying her.

And for existing cyclists, you can curry favour by pointing to a fellow bike lover who personifies something they aspire to, giving them reflected glory to bask in. For example, music lovers will be pleased to find that Elgar was a very keen cyclist. Conversely, for those who don't like music, you could cite Kraftwerk, and their 1983 single 'Tour de France'.

Here's a list of celebrities on wheels you can drop into conversations. There are plenty more, especially Hollywood actors (Michelle Pfeiffer, Russell Crowe, Arnold Schwarzenegger, to name a few; in fact, you can probably pick any Oscar nominee or sitcom starlet and maintain you saw them on a bike in a photoshoot).

Leo Tolstoy (1828–1910)

An inspiring example that it's never too late. The Russian author of *Anna Karenina* evidently took up cycling aged 67. On 18 April 1896, *Scientific American* reported that he 'now rides the wheel, much to the astonishment of the peasants on his estate'. There's no evidence, however, that *War and Peace* was inspired by rush-hour battles with Moscow taxis.

Mark Twain (1835–1910)

The American humorist learned to ride a penny-farthing in the early 1880s, when he was approaching 50. No doubt the experience inspired one of his most famous quotes, concluding his essay *Taming the Bicycle*: *'Get a bicycle. You will not regret it, if you live.'*

Sir Edward Elgar (1857–1934)

England's great romantic composer was a very keen cyclist from 1900 (when he was 43) to 1908, logging his extensive tours of the countryside around his Malvern home on OS maps. The oratorio masterpiece *'The Dream of Gerontius'* was probably composed while cycling, and there's no harm in claiming the tune to 'Land of Hope and Glory' was too. He gave up cycling partly because biking was 'less fun nowadays' thanks to all the new-fangled motor cars on the road, and partly because his older wife Alice, to his disappointment, preferred riding in one of these new-fangled motor cars over cycling trips to the pub in the rain.

Sir Arthur Conan Doyle (1859–1930)

The *Sherlock Holmes* author was a keen tricyclist, enthusing about his before- and after-work rides in the 18 January 1896 edition of *Scientific American*. He thought up many stories while riding. His detective creation knew about bikes, too, correctly identifying cyclists by their healthy glow and scuffed shoes. But Holmes made a mistake in *The Adventure of the Priory School,* thinking he could tell at a glance which way a bike had been going by the tyre marks. It is possible to work out the direction a bike was going from its tyre tracks, but it's a rather more complicated matter involving paper and pencil and a good knowledge of geometry, as does following a backstreet council-signed cycle route.

Gustav Holst (1874–1934)

A cheery example of how to behave when people treat you with contempt for being a cyclist. The English composer of 'The Planets' suite once biked down from London to the south coast to deliver a score to a colleague in person. His colleague's wife answered the door and, taking him for a common delivery man, frostily directed him to the back entrance. Unfazed, he complied. When his bemused conductor friend answered, Holst handed over the manuscript with a jokey 'delivery for you, sir!' Cite this as a good/bad example of Victorian social norms.

Albert Einstein (1879–1955)

It's often claimed that the physics visionary thought up the theory of relativity while riding his bike, even though there's no evidence he even had one when he was young. (He certainly did later, however, as a wild-haired professor at Princeton.) That needn't stop you asserting that his rule-changing stroke of genius – treating the speed of light as constant for any observer, which led to the whole bendy space-time, $e=mc^2$ thing – came from his front light working, but motorists still claiming they hadn't seen him. ('If Einstein had ridden without lights, maybe we wouldn't have nuclear bombs today…')

Sir Arthur Eddington (1882–1944)

The English astrophysicist devised the Eddington Number, E, a measure of a cyclist's long distance riding achievements, defined as the number of days in your life on which you cycled at least E miles. On his death, there had been 84 occasions on which he had cycled at least 84 miles, so he had a very respectable Eddington Number of 84. Come up with similar cycle-related ones of your own: Cake Number, Beer Number, Puncture Number, etc.

Eddy Merckx (1945–)

The only name you need remember from the world of racing, apart from Lance Armstrong (how can you forget the latter?). Generally considered 'the greatest', the race-hungry Belgian won 19 major titles in the 1960s and

1970s, including the Tour de France five times. For any other names that come up, the usual clichés probably apply: 'enigma', 'bit of a loner', 'incredible fighter – stats didn't do him justice', 'question marks over drug use miss the point', etc.

Sir Paul Smith (1946–)

The fashion designer is a keen cyclist, and his eponymous company has sponsored racing teams. Other image-makers who bike a lot include Jeff Banks (who has climbed all the major Alpine and Pyrenean cols) and Dame Vivienne Westwood, who has been spotted riding around south London with her fox terrier in the front basket; perhaps, given that bike theft is rife in the capital, it's more effective having a guard dog than a lock.

George W Bush (1946–)

Bush took up biking after a knee injury stopped him running. While attending the G8 summit in Scotland as US president in 2005, he managed to collide with a police officer while riding his mountain bike in the grounds of his hotel. Bush had fallen off his bike the year previously at his Texas ranch. It would be easy to make cheap cracks about Bush and compare his biking to his foreign policy prowess, so that's a very good reason to do so.

Lord Alan Sugar (1947–)

The acerbic entrepreneur used to buy and sell bikes before starting Amstrad, then got into cycling seriously in middle age. He rides a Pinarello and says gyms are 'brain-rottingly boring' – a concept he knows all about from some of the presentations he endures on the TV show *The Apprentice*.

Jon Snow (1947–)

In 2010, the *Daily Mail* ran a news item claiming they observed the Channel 4 news anchor and president of the CTC committing a string of offences while cycling in London, including jumping red lights and riding on the pavement. David Cameron was similarly 'exposed' by the *Daily Mirror* in 2008. Cite this as a cheap journalistic trick from tabloid rags who should be investigating proper stories, such as the fact that you once saw Jeremy Clarkson fail to indicate when changing lanes on the M25.

Jeremy Paxman (1950–)

The ferocious political interviewer clearly has the right attitude about everyday cycling: 'It is easily the quickest way around central London, faster than bus, tube or taxi. You can predict precisely how long every journey will take, regardless of traffic jams...' Speculate on what happens when a taxi driver takes him on in an argument ('Did you deliberately drive into my cycle lane? Answer the question. DID YOU OR DID YOU NOT DELIBERATELY DRIVE INTO MY CYCLE LANE?').

Robin Williams (1951–2014)

A riding chum of Lance Armstrong, the film star and comedian was a racing fan and bike collector (said to own over 50 road bikes). While working in New York in 2011, he was pulled over by the police for cycling on the pavement, but let off with a caution when they recognised him. Cite this as proof that he lived in the same world as normal cyclists, or in an invincible celebrity world of his own.

David Byrne (1952–)

The former Talking Heads musician has been getting around New York by bike since the 1980s, long before it was trendy. His book, *Bicycle Diaries,* came out in 2009; he has written regularly on cycling for *The New York Times*; and he auctioned one of his bikes to raise cash for the London Cycling Campaign (though a US resident, he is a British citizen). He is therefore an all-round 'good thing'. Depending on the age group you're trying to impress, you can cite other confirmed cycling musicians – John Lennon, Mick Jagger, Eric Clapton, Peter Gabriel, Sting, Jarvis Cocker, Paul McCartney, all of Kraftwerk, Jon Bon Jovi and Grateful Dead guitarist Bob Weir (the last two being mountain biking fanatics) – and there's nothing to stop you making up more.

Alexei Sayle (1952–)

The comedian and writer is a regular at Condor Cycles, the celeb cycling hangout in London, and once did a joy-of-A-to-B-cycling video for *The Guardian*. In it, he warmly recommends cycling home through the capital after a couple of drinks as the 'nearest you can get to flying'. Maintain this is either irresponsible, reckless and foolhardy, or in fact a jolly good suggestion for this evening.

Madonna (1958–)

Pictures of the muscle-bound entertainer riding her bike around London in an eye-catching outfit are a staple newspaper item for slow news days. Use this as evidence that cycling has gone mainstream, or is still stuck in a trivialised niche, as you like.

Will Self (1961–)

The writer and novelist is an everyday rider who once told London Cycling Campaign's magazine that, sadly, he felt unable to write the definitive bike novel 'that cycling so badly needs'. (It's possible he was not being entirely serious.) London's cyclo-lit fans groaned in disappointment. Everyone else sighed with relief.

Boris Johnson (1964–)

Former London mayor, famous for cycling everywhere in rumpled business suit. His tenure saw the high-profile Cycle Superhighways and Cycle Hire schemes implemented, which brought thousands of cyclists onto the streets – protesting at the poor and dangerous nature of the city's cycling facilities. He was once ticked off for riding down the temptingly smooth corkscrew ramp from the ground floor of City Hall down to the basement, which annoyed many cyclists – they all wanted a go too.

David Cameron (1966–)

Commuted to Westminster before and during his spell as British PM in 2010–2016. In 2006 it was revealed that his cycle commute to Westminster was followed by an official car, transporting his papers. In 2008 his

Scott bike was stolen from a supermarket, having been ineffectively locked; it was recovered but was stolen again in 2009 from his home. He proved as prone to losing referendums as he did bicycles.

Lance Armstrong (1971–)

What is there left to say? The only racer all non-fans have heard of, and the most (in)famous cyclist ever to appear on Oprah. The terrifyingly focused Texan famously beat testicular cancer to win the Tour de France consecutively between 1999 and 2005. He concentrated almost exclusively on the Tour, in contrast to widely-raced Merckx. Armstrong was continually dogged by allegations that he used performance-enhancing drugs, though he consistently denied doing so throughout his career. In June 2012 the US Anti-Doping Agency charged him with using banned substances, and in August 2012 it banned him from competition for life and stripped him of all of his titles since 1998. The USADA report concluded that Armstrong had devised 'the most sophisticated, professionalised and successful doping programme that sport has ever seen' (which is some achievement). In January 2013, Armstrong admitted doping in a TV interview with Oprah Winfrey. The whole sorry saga ranks as one of the most calamitous falls from grace in sporting history.

Minor bluffing point Armstrong appeared as himself in the Ben Stiller comedy *Dodgeball* in 2004, ironically as an iconic sporting figure espousing the importance of fortitude and resilience in the face of adversity.

Sir Bradley Wiggins (1980–)

One of Britain's most famous and most successful cyclists, first on the track and subsequently on road. In 2012 he became the first Briton (though born in Belgium) to win the Tour de France, and also won an Olympic gold in the time trial. It was one of his eight Olympic medals – more than any other Briton – five of them gold. He retired from pro cycling in 2016 and has recently taken up competitive rowing. His guitar-playing ability, stylish mod image, fluent French and outspoken personality endeared him to the public. However, his image was tarnished by a long, ultimately inconclusive, investigation into the dubious pharmaceutical contents of a jiffy bag delivered to the Team Sky doctor for his use in 2011. But then Sir Bradley has always been the complete package.

Mark Cavendish (1985–)

Like Wiggins, the Manxman has turned from track (winning the 2008 World Madison with Wiggins, for instance) to road (winning the green-jersey points classification in the 2011 Tour de France), where he is one of the world's fastest sprinters. Like Wiggins, he is a 'character': footballerish self-confidence and page three-model girlfriend, regular Twitter user, etc. – qualities much easier to research online and talk about than his racing techniques.

Chris Froome (1985–)

In 2013, Froome followed Wiggins by winning the Tour de France, another Briton born abroad (in Kenya).

Thanks to the ruthlessly competitive Team Sky he won again in 2015, 2016 and 2017, also becoming the first British rider to win the Vuelta d'España that year. His status as Britain's most successful male racing cyclist was marred by an 'adverse analytical finding' after that Vuelta which showed an illegally high level of the (legal) asthma drug Salbutamol in his blood. With so many grey areas, you can hold any opinion about Froome from anti ('clearly dodgy – how come he suddenly improved in his mid-20s with jiffy-bag merchants Team Sky?') to pro ('clearly clean – the improvement was due to his bilharzia undisputably being cured, the Salbutamol was legal and recognised and the dose a doctor's screw-up') and nobody can disprove you.

Mr and Mrs Kenny

Britain's golden track-cycling couple: in 2016 Jason Kenny (born 1988, six Olympic golds, level with fellow track cyclist Sir Chris Hoy of Scotland) married Laura Trott (born 1992, four Olympic golds, UK cycling's new poster-girl after Victoria Pendleton). They live in a cottage in Cheshire, which would have finished 19th in the 2016 Olympics medal table if it had been a country. If their young son cycles to school he will have little excuse for being late.

ß

97% of the time, people won't quibble with statistics, however dubious, that happen to confirm what they believe.

LIES, DAMNED LIES, AND...

26 SOURCED FACTS AND FIGURES YOU CAN USE TO PROVE ANYTHING*

Quoting statistics is a quick and dirty way to support any argument. Experts estimate that of all figures quoted, 35% are made up and false, 55% are essentially true but unconvincingly sourced, and the remaining 20% contain some sort of glaring arithmetical error.**

But it's an effective way, too. 97% of the time, people won't quibble with statistics, however dubious, that happen to confirm what they believe. So here are 26 genuine facts and figures that you can use at any time to prove pretty much anything, as our 'therefores' demonstrate.

*For sources go to bluffers.com/cycling-stats/.
**Source: *The Bluffer's Guide to Cycling*, 2018, p101.

Where are all the bikes?

Government figures show that there are 34 million motor vehicles on the road in Britain (and about

THE BLUFFER'S GUIDE TO CYCLING

the same number of licensed drivers) of which 28.4 million are cars. The CTC reckons there are 23 million bikes, and that 43% of people over the age of five have one. However, *Bike Week* says that only 14% of bike owners actually use one regularly. Therefore, bicycles are nearly as numerous as cars – you just don't see any of them as they're hidden in garages.

Helmets are dangerous...

After Australia made cycle helmets compulsory in 1992, the numbers of head injuries sustained by cyclists went down – but not as much as cycling did. Similar effects have been observed in other places where helmet-wearing has been made mandatory. Therefore, making helmets compulsory actually makes head injuries more likely.

...but good for pedestrians...

However, researchers in Victoria, examining the data from Western Australia, decided that helmets were effective at preventing head injuries for cyclists. Over the same period, such injuries declined similarly for pedestrians. Therefore, cycle helmets protect pedestrians against head injuries, even though they aren't wearing them.

...while wigs are safer...

Researcher Ian Walker in 2006 found that motor vehicles gave helmeted cyclists less room when passing than those unhelmeted. However, when he wore a long blonde wig, they gave him more room. Therefore, a long blonde wig is safer than a helmet.

...and pelotons safer still

After looking at the effect of cycling numbers on accident rates over many countries, researchers concluded that the total number of pedestrians or cyclists struck by motorists varies with the 0.4th power of the amount of walking or cycling. In other words, roughly speaking, if cycling levels double, the risk of an individual having an accident falls by a third; if it halves, the risk doubles. However, decision-making gets slower and harder the larger a group becomes, with odd numbers better. Therefore, to balance safety, without wasting too much time deciding which pub or cafe to visit, cycle in a group size of three, five or seven.

Visors make helmets hotter

On most cycle helmets, the visor meant to block the sun from your eyes soaks up heat from the sun, and sets up an airflow which takes hot air to the scalp, making the helmet feel hotter than one without a visor. Therefore, a visor most likely makes the helmet hotter in sunny weather.

Cyclists stay young

A 1986 study of male middle-aged factory workers found that cycling was the single lifestyle factor with the strongest health benefit: those who cycled regularly had a level of fitness equivalent to non-cyclists 10 years younger; even occasional cyclists had a five-year advantage. A separate study reckons that heavy smoking reduces life expectancy by nine years. Therefore, regular cyclists can smoke heavily and still live a year longer than the stationary (not that we'd recommend it).

Bicycle 'road tax' would be 1p per year...

According to internationally accepted figures, the cost of damage done to road surfaces by vehicles is proportional to four to the power of the axle weight. So a car weighing, say, 900kg doesn't do 10 times as much damage as someone on a bike totalling 90kg: it does 10x10x10x10, or 10,000, times as much. Therefore, if 'road tax' were set to reflect damage done, and drivers paid £100 per year, cyclists would pay 1p.

...no, it would be 0p per year...

'Road tax' is really vehicle excise duty (VED), a tax on tailpipe emissions. Low-emission vehicles such as electric cars or the Volkswagen Golf 1.6 TDI BlueMotion 105 are zero-rated for VED. Many other vehicles or drivers are zero-rated too: police cars, disabled drivers, tractors and The Queen. Therefore, as a zero-emission vehicle, a bicycle would pay no VED.

...anyway cyclists pay more 'road tax' than non-cyclists

According to government responses to a parliamentary question in May 2011 based on the National Travel Survey, 83% of cyclists have access to a car, compared to 82% for the general population. Therefore, cyclists pay more 'road tax' than non-cyclists.

London is greener than East Anglia

Government statistics indicate that 25% of households nationally don't have access to a car. The most car-free region is London: in the boroughs, 43% of households survive without one. In East Anglia the motorless figure is only 16%. Therefore, London is more environmentally friendly than East Anglia.

Bike facilities are cheap
The cost of one mile of urban motorway could alternatively buy 150 miles of cycle paths, 10,000 miles of cycle lanes, or 100 well-designed 20mph zones. Therefore, one mile of cycle lane would buy 6 inches of motorway, with both distances taking about the same amount of time to cover during rush hour.

Best way to kill someone
The number of pedestrians and cyclists killed on UK roads each year is the same as all murders. However, dangerous and careless drivers who kill them are routinely punished less harshly than other criminals who cause similar deaths without intent. Therefore, if you want to kill someone, running over them apparently by accident is the best way to a shorter sentence.

Eco hot water? That's your lot
In the USA, car parks occupy a total area larger than the size of Puerto Rico. Most are unused the majority of the time, and serve as large black asphalt heat magnets, warming the atmosphere. Some companies are experimenting to see if they can heat water in pipes underneath and use it for domestic and office heating. Therefore, car parks might be a valuable green resource.

Ditch hire bikes, pay London cyclists
Public subsidy per passenger kilometre for travellers in

London is 6p for buses and 1p for the tube. For users of the Santander Cycle Hire scheme – which apparently generates on average 20,000 journeys a day of 10-30 minutes and will use £140 million of public money over six years – the figure is more like 75p. Therefore, it would be cheaper to pay cyclists say 50p a mile to ride their own bikes in central London.

Car commutes grind to a halt

A 2012 survey by carmaker Citroën suggested that rush-hour drivers in British cities spend an average 25 minutes of every hour stationary, up from 20 minutes five years previously. The figure for London is 36 minutes per hour. Cyclists, largely immune to jams, keep going at a steady 10-15mph. Therefore, poster advertising should not be aimed at cyclists, but at motorists, who have plenty of time to read it.

Cycling member benefits

Men who cycle three to five hours a week have 30% less risk of being impotent, said a 2003 Harvard study. However, really serious cyclists may suffer lower fertility: in another study, Spanish triathletes doing 180 miles per week saw a (temporary and reversible) drop in viable sperm from the average 10% to a borderline-infertile 4%, an effect not seen in those swimming or running only. Therefore, cycling is good for your sex life, but only in moderation, like chocolate and beer.

Dutch courage

'Modal share' – the proportion of trips made by bike as

opposed to other forms of transport – is low in the UK: 1% by distance and 2% of all journeys. The figures for cars are 62% and 78%. Certain cities do better: in York, 19% of trips are made by bike; in Cambridge, 28%. In Groningen in the Netherlands – often cited as the developed-world city with the highest proportion of cycling – around 40% of all trips are made by bike, compared to a Dutch average of 27%. Therefore, Cambridge is better than the Netherlands for cycling.

Is high-visibility clothing worth it?

A 2009 study from Australia found no significant benefit of high-visibility over dark clothing for avoiding accidents at night. A 2011 study from Texas claimed that helmets mitigated head injuries for the sober, but not for alcohol drinkers. Therefore, if you've had too much to drink, don't waste your time putting on a helmet or a high-visibility jacket – buy another drink instead, as it won't make things any worse.

Walking v cycling

Cycling is safe. You can cycle 25 million miles before you can expect to be killed – about the same distance as for pedestrians walking. However, it would take you 700 years cycling 100 miles a day to reach that figure, during which time you're bound to collide with said pedestrian at some point.

Bike theft

Around 115,000 bikes are reported stolen each year in Britain, though many more thefts go unreported:

the total number of thefts is thought to be more like 500,000. Less than 5% are returned to their owners. Experts recommend using two locks and spending 30% of the value of the bike on them.

Therefore, if you have a £3,000 Pinarello road bike, you must spend £900 on locks.

Boom, boom

In 1949, one-third of all distances people covered was by bike. Since the 1960s it has fluctuated around 1%. On-road cycling levels are increasing very slightly (up 10% in the last decade, though inner London has seen levels double in that time, mainly because the same people are cycling more). Off-road cycling has increased twice as much as on-road, but that's still a tiny number of miles. Therefore, any cycling boom the media tries to talk about is more of a muffled thud.

Criminal practices

According to a 2011 BBC presentation on road accidents, a large percentage of those involved in fatal collisions have a criminal record: 41% of lorry drivers, 35% of cyclists and van drivers, 30% of pedestrians, and 21% of car drivers (compared with the background rate of 8%). Therefore, calls for the licensing of cyclists to prevent accidents are misguided: far better to license criminals.

Give cyclists more holidays

The same presentation showed a spike in cycle deaths during morning and evening weekday rush hours. Therefore, it's not cycling that's dangerous – it's going to work.

It's a bit rich

Psychologists at the University of California, Berkeley, found that the richer a driver is, and the more expensive the car, the more likely it is they will cut up other road users and not stop for pedestrians. Therefore, people on bikes are just nicer and more polite.

How to be law-abiding

Even though 83% of drivers say they break the speed limit regularly, 92% of them believe they are 'law-abiding', according to an RAC poll; while an IAM survey showed that 88% of drivers believe cyclists 'should improve their behaviour'. (This despite Transport for London data showing that the same percentage of drivers jump red lights as cyclists: about 16%.) Therefore, the best way to be considered law-abiding is not to cycle responsibly, but to drive a car instead.

Many legal professionals cycle. So, if there's someone in the group with a top-end Brompton who starts citing case law, best wait till they've gone.

WHEELS OF JUSTICE

Sounding like a legal expert (when in fact you survive on a handful of facts off the top of your head), knowing where to look things up if challenged, and bluster – are all very good skills to develop. Lawyers use them all the time.

Cyclists are always wondering about the legality of what they've just done, so here's a guide to UK law as it applies to bikes. It will make you sound authoritative the next time the topic arises. Some words of warning: many legal professionals cycle. So, if there's someone in the group with a top-end Brompton who starts citing case law, best wait till they've gone. They'll be much better at bluffing than you – they're good enough to charge for it. What follows is for entertainment and general information purposes only. It should not be taken as legal advice. There is of course no substitute for a reliable, competent lawyer. If you ever find one, let us know who he or she is.

PAVEMENT CYCLING

This is a subject that gets most people steamed up, and as far as the law is concerned, is not a straightforward one. Pedestrians often do not know where they stand, though it's usually in the middle of a cycle track, texting.

First, the word 'pavement' has no legal definition, so you can claim that anyone using it has no idea what they're talking about. (It's called 'sidewalk' in the USA. 'Pavement' there means 'paved road', though there are quite a lot of drivers there who think cycling on a road is a civil outrage too.)

It's called cycling on the footway – the strip alongside a road meant for pedestrians – and it's illegal (unless there's a sign saying you're allowed to).

Cycling on a footpath (where there's not a road – promenades, parks, shopping precincts, or in the countryside) is only illegal if there's a sign saying so. Otherwise you can only be done for trespass on a footpath (for which you can't be prosecuted – only taken to a civil court for the damage you've done, which will probably be none). You're allowed to push a bike anywhere, footway or footpath.

Cycling on a bridleway (a path open to walkers, cyclists, horses and brides, but not cars) is fine. Cycling on a pedestrianised street just because you need access is not. (Anyway it's probably dangerous, because of all the delivery lorries and vans that need access.)

A cycle track is somewhere you're specifically allowed to cycle but cars aren't. It's usually recognisable by signage, often by red or green tarmac, and the fact that it stops abruptly after 50 metres and dumps you back in the traffic. On a split pedestrian/cycling track, the pedestrian side remains a footpath and you can't cycle on it – if you can tell which side it actually is. You have to cycle 'considerately' on such tracks – it's an offence not to – which means giving way to walkers, even if they're on your bit. Pedestrians walking inconsiderately are not committing an offence, and anyway you couldn't trace them if they did, which may be an argument for having them all licensed and insured.

'Cycle path' is a bit vague and best avoided. In fact cycle paths as a whole are vague and generally best avoided – the road is usually quicker, simpler and not full of broken lager bottles.

If you are caught cycling where you shouldn't be, a uniformed officer may give you a fixed penalty notice and a £30 fine. Often, utilising the sort of confusion outlined previously, there are loopholes which any decent lawyer can use to have your penalty dropped, charging you only a few hundred pounds. Cycle inconsiderately and you could end up with a fine of £1,000, though again a competent lawyer could fight this for you for only a few grand.

You don't have to use off-road cycle tracks or facilities – you're perfectly entitled to stay on the road, whatever The Highway Code tries to tell you (they 'can make your journey safer', it claims, which is like saying you 'can win money in online casinos').

On-road cycle lanes come in two types: advisory, marked by a dotted line, which cars don't have to stay out of, and are always too narrow and of little use; and compulsory, marked by a solid line, which cars do have to stay out of, and are always too narrow and of little use. Despite the names, cyclists don't have to stay inside either of them. Another name for cycle lanes is car parking spaces.

SPEEDING

Speed limits only apply to motor vehicles, not bikes. So cycling at 45mph in a 30mph limit, like boasting about it in a pub, is not an offence by itself but probably not a great idea.

Anyway, there are cases – very rare, but one was reported in Cambridge in 2007 – of cyclists who incur the wrath of police in these or similar circumstances and are charged under arcane nineteenth-century laws such as 'riding furiously' or 'wanton and furious driving'. So our advice is: if you do break the speed limit on a bike, don't collide with a policeman.

RED-LIGHT JUMPING

It's always an offence to jump a normal, round, red traffic signal, though it does have a remarkable side effect – you suddenly stop being invisible to traffic.

How legal it is to get off at a red, walk a bit, jump on your bike and ride on, is one of those imponderables, though one thing is certain – lawyers on either side would convince you they'd win your case.

However, on a shared cycle-pedestrian path (e.g., at a crossing), it's not an offence to jump the red-man sign that tells walkers to stop. So there's one red light you can legally ride past.

DRINK AND DRUGS...

Is drink-cycling against the law? It's a topic much debated, especially by cyclists in the pub wondering if they should order another round of drinks. The answer is, of course, yes. (And also yes, drink-cycling is indeed illegal.)

In theory, being 'drunk in charge' of a bicycle (and in fact, being a drunk pedestrian) is an offence, but is never enforced. It's also an offence to ride when unfit through drink or drugs on a road or 'other public place' (such as canal towpaths, which make for an entertaining challenge for the homeward-bound pub-goer). If found guilty of cycling 'dangerously' you could be fined up to £2,500, which would make your evening out look rather more expensive, unless you'd been in a central London cocktail bar.

You can't have your breath, blood or urine tested, and in practice a police officer will tell a wobbling overindulger to get off and push home rather than to go through all the paperwork, especially when drunks are involved. Bike theft at country pubs during evening-spin season is rife, so it's a good idea to get a good combination lock – if you're too drunk to remember the code then you shouldn't be cycling home anyway.

...AND ROCK AND ROLL

It's not an offence to ride while listening to music on your iPod, though most cyclists think it's a pretty silly thing to do. After all, you can't hope to concentrate on that Shostakovich string quartet as closely as you should be if you're riding the North Circular at rush hour.

TWO ON A BIKE

Illegal unless the bike is specifically designed to take an extra person (with a child seat, for instance). Giving someone a 'backie' is an offence. If you're under the influence of soft drugs, it's doubly illegal, and called a 'wacky backie'.

UNICYCLES

Are either subject to exactly the same rules as bikes, so can't be ridden on the pavement, for example (Statutory Instrument 1994 No 1519), or are specifically not 'bicycles', so can be (Statutory Instrument 2003 No 1101). In other words, no one's sure until a test case comes along, but it's a rare unicyclist who could afford such litigation.

HELMETS

Only two countries in the world enforce a legal requirement for all cyclists to wear helmets everywhere all the time– Australia and New Zealand. Several others make helmets compulsory for children (which is what helmets are designed to cope with – a child falling off a stationary bike onto tarmac, not a moving adult being hit by a car).

In the USA and Canada, the situation varies by state and county, though, overall, helmets are usually not required for adults. Spain has the weirdest legislation: helmets are compulsory except in towns, uphill, or if it's hot.

In the UK – like France, Germany, and the safest and best countries in the world for cycling, the Netherlands and Denmark – there's no requirement to wear one, unless you're a cycling politician scared of losing votes.

No cyclist compensated in a conventional UK road accident has ever had their damages reduced through not wearing a helmet. (If anyone disagrees, your defence hinges on the word 'conventional'.)

Dismiss any reported comments by cyclists, nurses, coroners, judges or police officers about helmets: unless they have conducted controlled scientific tests, assert that their views are unfounded and prejudiced. There's only one reliable opinion on helmets, backed up by research, experience and wisdom – yours.

The effect of helmets on a conversation is still being debated. Some cyclists believe that telling people you don't wear a helmet can harm or even kill a conversation, while others believe it is perfectly safe.

LIGHTS

Bikes ridden at night (on roads, bridleways, cycle tracks, etc.) must have a front white and rear red light, which can be either steady or (since the law was changed in 2005) flashing. They must also have a red rear reflector and, if manufactured after 1985 when bikes presumably became more night-coloured, reflectors on the pedals – an impossibility for many road bikes, which have tiny clipless pedals.

In practice, the public do not write letters of complaint to local newspapers demanding that something be done about the menace of cyclists whose pedal reflectors do not conform to British Standard 6102/2.

Curiously, in Germany, lights must be fitted to a bike all the time, even in daylight.

BELLS

Not required by law on a bike in Britain (though they are in Northern Ireland, perhaps thanks to the region's strong musical heritage). They used to be compulsory on cycles when sold new, but recent clearing out of red-tape legislation dispensed with that.

Bells have been rendered largely useless as drivers can't hear them over their mobile, and pedestrians can't hear them over their iPods. If they're listening to rap, then shouting obscenities at them is similarly pointless.

BRAKES

The front and rear wheel must have independent braking systems. A fixed-wheel bike doesn't need a back brake, as the pedals can act as one, but there must be a front brake too – fixies without one are illegal, which only adds to the mystique. It was on such an illegal bike that a certain Charlie Alliston crashed into, and killed, a pedestrian in London in 2016. He got 18 months in prison.

The same goes for bikes with back-pedal brakes – where the rear brake is not applied by a lever, but by a quick backwards push on the pedals. These are popular on the continent but rare in the UK, making the phrase 'back-pedalling' – as in 'retracting a statement or view' – puzzling to non-cyclists: back-pedal on a normal bike and it just carries on forwards as your feet spin round on the freewheel. This can lead you away from cycle regulations and into politics, if you want to start an argument.

MOBILE PHONES

It's not an offence to use one while riding – to text a friend, or perhaps ring one of those 'How Am I Driving?' numbers on the side of a lorry to complain – but it presumably could count against you in the event of an accident. At least you'd be able to call the CTC legal helpline right away.

FUTURE SPECULATION

Extrapolate the effect of any social trends you see on future law-making – online democracy and safety concerns, for example. ('There'll be emotive TV appeals by parents of children involved in tragic accidents demanding compulsory helmets, even though they haven't got a clue about the issues. The impressionable, feckless public will agree with one-click online legislation, and by 2025, in every country you'll have to have helmets, elbow guards, knee pads and bike-mounted fire sprinklers. Except the Netherlands, which won't have any cycle tracks above sea level left.')

If Microsoft or Apple had invented bicycles, they'd have seven wheels and four saddles

TECHNOLOGICAL PROGRESS

Technological progress has generally served cyclists, not the other way round. If Microsoft or Apple had invented bicycles, they'd have seven wheels and four saddles. When you turned the handlebars, the wheels wouldn't actually go that way, but the direction they thought you ought to go. You'd be stopped mid-ride and be forced to update the saddle settings that were perfectly good as they were. When you braked, you'd get a message saying 'You've applied the brake. Do you want to (a) slow down (b) stop (c) cancel?' And they'd cost twenty thousand pounds for a one-user licence.

Thankfully, the basic ingredients of a bike are simple, easy to control, and haven't changed much for over a century – part of what makes cycling so attractive. Many innovations – usually the ones trumpeted on Kickstarter – can be safely dismissed as impractical gimmicks that fail to beat common sense ('Motion-triggered theft alarms? Better to simply lock your bike next to a more valuable, more tempting one...').

But bike manufacturers are always trying something new. Typically, technology developed for high-end racing – such as carbon fibre frames, disc brakes or electronic shifting – filters down to the the mainstream. So it's worth knowing about. If anyone mentions an exciting new development and you don't want to sound ignorant, you can always try the line 'sounds fantastic, no doubt will be standard in future, but I'm waiting for the price to come down'. You'll never be far wrong.

FRAME MATERIAL

Bikes have been made out of all sorts, such as bamboo (either dismiss as 'for novelty hire-bikes only' or praise as 'light, strong, natural, rides very nicely') or plastic (Sweden's 1980s ramshackle and unsuccessful Itera). The following are the four standard materials for frames and forks. Champion one of them, according to your desired image:

Carbon fibre
Very light and strong, but only in one direction, and when it fails it fails irretrievably. Carbon forks are common and can absorb shocks well, such as when you find out how much a frame/fork combination costs. Choice for quality road bikes and racers. *Image*: High-achieving, front-line, perhaps temperamental.

Steel
Flexible, strong, cheap, weldable. Cliché justification

is that unlike the other materials, a steel frame 'can be repaired by a blacksmith or mechanic even in the remotest developing-country village'. In practice this never really happens, but it sounds good, and suggests you have toured excitingly far away, and have met a blacksmith. Choice therefore for touring bikes, commuting, general bikes. *Image*: Solid, reliable, down-to-earth.

Aluminium

Light, stiff but less strong than steel; inexpensive, doesn't corrode, and can be repaired (but not by blacksmiths). Good general-purpose frame material for variety of bikes. *Image*: Straightforward, untarnished, regular person.

Titanium

Niche material and engineering skills required, expensive, very light and durable, doesn't corrode, comfy. Aspirational material for tourers and many other types of bike. *Image*: Connoisseur, high standards but expects special treatment.

STRAVA

The app of choice for serious cyclists with many millions of users worldwide, Strava uses GPS to record the route of your ride. You upload it to the website and can compare your times for 'segments' against other cyclists: being fastest for a segment earns you the title 'King/Queen of the Mountains'. Also has a social media aspect – 'Facebook for cyclists', with 'kudos' the Strava equivalent of a 'like'.

Everyone will expect you to be on it, so to avoid being asked to link up with others, claim to use it on private settings only, so that only you can see your segment times ('it's for me, not to impress other people...'). If you do go public, be sure to ride very obscure routes so you can easily claim King or Queen status. Or you could simply try dissing it ('Why do its users insist on posting up their latest segment to Facebook? I go there specifically to avoid the Strava bores...') and make a random case for one of its less popular rivals ('Mapmyride is more reliable, Endomondo is easier to use, and haven't you tried Trailforks for MTBing...?').

The Strava equivalent for turbo trainers, enabling you to 'race' at home against another user remotely, is Zwift. You can have any opinion you like about it, as anyone who actually uses Zwift will be at home, racing someone in the US.

GPS

Smartphone-sized handlebar device that uses GPS to show where you are on a map, and gives you directions; Garmin is the best-known brand. Pretty standard, so nobody will quiz you in depth about it if you want to imply that you use it. However, some people might be impressed by the 'pure old-fashioned cycling' image: 'GPS? I ask directions from real people, much more sociable! And I use proper paper maps that give you an overview! And if I need an annoying little chirp telling me we're lost, my partner can do that...', etc.

ELECTRONIC SHIFTING

The latest top-end technology for changing gear, which is faster and more precise than conventional mechanics (especially if it uses wireless instead of cables). Decide whether you're anti ('no sense of feel, batteries can run out, hideously expensive') or pro ('so much more efficient, I was instantly converted to the Di2, if only I could afford it...').

DISC BRAKES

Increasingly popular, these work by pads pinching an exposed metal disc fixed to your wheel hubs. They come in two types, mechanical and hydraulic. Hydraulic ones are more powerful, but more complex and must be full of liquid to work, like some riders.

Disc brakes are more effective than normal rim brakes and stay grippy even in mud and the wet. They're increasingly found on all sorts of bikes, but have proved particularly popular with mountain bikers as they still work even if the wheel itself gets knocked out of shape, or even if the rider does.

There's no point in pretending that you know everything about cycling – nobody does – but if you've got this far and you've absorbed at least a modicum of the information and advice contained within these pages, then you will almost certainly know more than 99% of the rest of the human race about what it involves, how it can be good for your health, how it can be bad for your health, why cyclists are often misunderstood, and why – on the whole – cycling is generally a good thing (for life, the universe, and everything).

What you now do with this information is up to you, but here's a suggestion: be confident about your new-found knowledge, see how far it takes you, but above all have fun using it. You are now a bona fide expert in the art of bluffing about the world's most efficient form of transport. Just try not to fall off.

GLOSSARY

Aerobars *n pl* Handlebar extensions enabling arms-flat-forward, streamlined riding position popular with triathletes; (with capital 'A') chocolate snack popular with tourers.

Bonk *n and vb* Real or feigned sudden energy collapse while riding, instantly remedied by consumption of chocolate or cake.

Boris bike *n vulg* Hire cycle from London's Santander-sponsored scheme, named after Mayor Boris Johnson. Big, solid and funny-looking, but soon becomes tiresome, with progress slow. Same for the bike.

Butterfly bars *n pl* Figure-eight-shaped handlebars used by some touring cyclists, and like real butterflies, much more difficult to get hold of than you'd think.

Clipless pedals *n pl* Pedals with clips (but for cleats on your shoes, not toe clips); other oxymorons include 'thief-resistant lock', 'rainproof jacket' and 'cycle facility'.

Crash *n* Incident reported by newspapers as 'collision' between 'cyclist' (never 'cycle') and 'vehicle' (never 'driver'); breakdown of newspaper's server when deluged by angry cyclist emails complaining about this implied victim-blaming.

Door zone *n* Dangerous area immediately alongside row of parked cars where abruptly opened doors can knock cyclists off into passing traffic, and therefore where most cycle lanes are painted.

Dropout *n* Bit of the frame that lets your wheels drop out easily; system-dodger who becomes a bike mechanic or courier.

Drops *n pl* The lower curved bits of road-bike handlebars, enabling streamlined riding position; medication to relieve resulting neck pain.

Face plant *n* Falling off (usually mountain bike) face-first onto ground, resulting in enough facial mud to grow flowers.

Fixie *n* Fixed-wheel bike (i.e., single speed, no freewheel, even no brakes) that can be hard to stop – like owners talking about them.

Granny *adj* Lowest gear, easiest to pedal ('granny gear', 'granny cog'); sometimes engaged out of reluctant duty, as with real grannies.

Gravel/adventure bike Jack-of-all-trades compromise bike: can do commuting, road runs, touring, off-road trails, etc., which allows you to have one bike instead of five, thus defeating the point.

Hardtail *n* Mountain bike with front but not rear suspension; difficult story about how you can't afford the full-suspension model this particular downhill route really requires.

LBS *abbr* 'local bike shop'. Praise them all for great service and knowledgeable staff, and lament their struggles against cheaper internet stores – before quietly ordering all your gear online like everyone else.

Left hook *n* Driving movement in which a vehicle overtakes you then immediately turns left across you; type of punch delivered by furious cyclist to driver afterwards.

Mechanical doping *n* Hidden electric motor giving illicit help to racers, using technology that pushes the envelope – one full of used banknotes, slipped from rider to mechanic.

Peloton *n* Huddled group of road cyclists minimising both collective wind resistance and chance of car behind overtaking.

Primary position *n* Riding line in the middle of the traffic lane, recommended for safety, and for learning

new swear words from impatient drivers behind you. *cf*
Secondary position In the gutter – less dirty language
but more dirty trousers.

Quietways *n* Signed low-traffic backstreet cycle routes
through London ('Q1', 'Q6', etc.); so called because
councils are reticent to say how much they cost for such
modest results.

Rail trail *n* Scenic former railway made into level,
smooth, continuous cycle path; dull former railway
made into muddy, rough cycle path interrupted by road
crossings and housing estates.

Rapha Ultra-stylish and ultra-pricey cycle-clothing
brand whose wearers always claim to have 'bought in
the sale'.

RLJ *abbr 'red-light jumper'* Cyclist invisible to the public
until they ignore a red traffic light, when they become
All Cyclists.

Single track *n* Off-road cycle track only wide enough
for one cyclist, typically difficult and rough. *cf* Easy and
smooth urban paved cycle tracks, which are also only
wide enough for one cyclist.

SMIDSY *abbr* Acronym for 'Sorry mate I didn't see
you', archetypal motorist's excuse for near-miss with
6ft cyclist with high-visibility jacket and flashing rock
concert LEDs.

Tubeless tyres *n pl* Car-style, inner-tube-free tyres that require special wheels; associated with high pressure, such as that of worrying what happens when they puncture.

Turbo trainer *n* Device enabling you to ride your bike stationary indoors, hence good for winter training; by adding an electric motor, you can train without even getting on the bike, and perhaps go for a ride instead.

Winter bike *n* Robust second-string bike: to avoid the best road bike deteriorating from use in inhospitable weather, the 'winter bike' is the one that is unridden instead.

A BIT MORE BLUFFING...